God's
Glory
Revealed

God's Glory Revealed

52 Devotionals

Randy L Allen

NELLA PUBLISHING HOUSE
A division of Nella Limited Liability Company
Tuscaloosa, Alabama

Cover: Sea of Galilee from Capernaum, Israel.

www.RandyLAllen.com

ISBN   978-1-7344159-0-2

First Edition: April 2020

Contents

Introduction

1.	God is With You	1
2.	Believe, Seek & See	8
3.	Seek First	13
4.	Praying the Psalms	18
5.	God's Protection	23
6.	God Heals Kennedy	27
7.	Revelation Through the Ordinary	32
8.	God Works Through People	36
9.	Separate Yet Blended	41
10.	Mercy Not Sacrifice	46
11.	Mercy Not Sacrifice – Part II	51
12.	Glory Through Suffering	56
13.	Releasing Our Children to God	62
14.	God Incarnate	68
15.	Eyes to See	74
16.	Awesome Yet Routine	78
17.	Called to Compassion	83
18.	Holy Living Sacrifice	88
19.	Stumbling Blocks	94
20.	Strongholds	99
21.	Divine Power to Destroy Strongholds	105
22.	A Prayer for Unity	110
23.	A Prayer for Unity – Part II	115
24.	Service Begets Wholeness	123
25.	Prepared for Service	127
26.	From Suffering to Glory	132
27.	From Suffering to Glory – Part II	136
28.	From Suffering to Glory – Part III	140
29.	From Suffering to Glory – Part IV	144
30.	The Word	149

31. Instructions for Life 153

32. Jesus Warns 158

33. Apostles Warn 165

34. Paul's Farewell 172

35. A Heart to Know God 178

36. Peace Be With You 184

37. Touching the Fringe 188

38. Seizing the Power of God 193

39. Progressing to Childlike 198

40. Lives of Our Words 204

41. Enemy's Attack 210

42. "Do Whatever He Tells You" 216

43. New Life in Christ 220

44. Trust, Faith & Peace 225

45. Sifted Like Wheat 230

46. God Provides Abundance 235

47. Trusting Future Provision 239

48. Saying Thank You 245

49. Do Not Worry 249

50. Prayer Inhibits Temptation 256

51. Pruning Branches 260

52. Peace in Christ 263

About the Author 270

Notes 272

INTRODUCTION

As a boy, while standing alone in the sun-filled atrium between the sanctuary and fellowship hall enjoying quiet stillness, I felt God's unmistakable presence. I knew He was with me, welcoming me, loving me. Over the next twenty-five years I did my best to forget the encounter. Without even considering a career in ministry, I earned an engineering degree and a law degree and quickly jumped into the grind of life as an associate in a law firm in Denver.

Through a series of seemingly unrelated events, I found myself stranded in an empty concourse waiting after a canceled flight. I finished all the work I had in my bag and read two newspapers and in bored desperation I dug through my briefcase searching for something to read and I found, tucked in the bottom of a rarely used pocket, a thin copy of the New Testament that a man had handed me months earlier as I walked along a street in Denver. With my left thumb I fanned the pages from the back, saw the word Revelation and stopped to read. Sitting there in an empty concourse, I felt apprehensive wondering what people would think of me if they saw me reading the Bible, but I continued and as I read I felt God's unmistakable presence once again. His living word came to life. Since that day I have continued reading His holy word and He continues to respond.

A few years ago I started writing a weekly devotional to help launch our church app. Each Wednesday we posted a new devotional through the app and members of our congregation expressed appreciation for the weekly offering. As people outside our congregation began asking for the devotionals, we gradually took steps to make the weekly offerings more accessible, including weekly emails, a standalone website and now a book.

Before launching into devotionals, it might be appropriate to mention the cover photo. A few years ago I stood on the Capernaum shore not far from Peter's home gazing over the Sea of Galilee. I was suddenly overcome with the realization that Peter, other disciples and Jesus stood on the same shore admiring the same scene. I imagined Peter sipping his tea while smelling the sea air, feeling the air warm as the sun rose above the sea, mending his nets, tending to the day's catch. I imagined Jesus standing on the same shore as He asked Peter to put away his nets and follow Him, and later instructed Peter and others to cast their net on the other side of the boat, leading to a miraculous catch. I imagined sailors on the sea terrified by a storm that ceased at Jesus' command. I imagined Jesus walking on that very body of water, teaching from a nearby boat and healing a demoniac somewhere near the hills across the water. God's holy word tells us that the Word became flesh. As I stood there, taking it all in, a great deal of His word shifted from intellectual to tangible. I took the photo to remind me of the moment.

I pray that the devotionals in this book will supplement your practice of seeking God the Father, Jesus Christ and the Holy Spirit through prayer, studying and meditating on Scripture, and private and public worship.

1

GOD IS WITH YOU

WHEN MOSES HAD FINISHED SPEAKING ALL THESE WORDS TO ALL ISRAEL, HE SAID TO THEM: "I AM NOW ONE HUNDRED TWENTY YEARS OLD. I AM NO LONGER ABLE TO GET ABOUT, AND THE LORD HAS TOLD ME, 'YOU SHALL NOT CROSS OVER THIS JORDAN.' THE LORD YOUR GOD HIMSELF WILL CROSS OVER BEFORE YOU. HE WILL DESTROY THESE NATIONS BEFORE YOU, AND YOU SHALL DISPOSSESS THEM. JOSHUA ALSO WILL CROSS OVER BEFORE YOU, AS THE LORD PROMISED. THE LORD WILL DO TO THEM AS HE DID TO SIHON AND OG, THE KINGS OF THE AMORITES, AND TO THEIR LAND, WHEN HE DESTROYED THEM. THE LORD WILL GIVE THEM OVER TO YOU AND YOU SHALL DEAL WITH THEM IN FULL ACCORD WITH THE COMMAND THAT I HAVE GIVEN TO YOU. BE STRONG AND BOLD; HAVE NO FEAR OR DREAD OF THEM, BECAUSE IT IS THE LORD YOUR GOD WHO GOES WITH YOU; HE WILL NOT FAIL YOU OR FORSAKE YOU."

THEN MOSES SUMMONED JOSHUA AND SAID TO HIM IN THE SIGHT OF ALL ISRAEL: "BE STRONG AND BOLD, FOR YOU ARE THE ONE WHO WILL GO WITH THIS PEOPLE INTO THE LAND THAT THE LORD HAS SWORN TO THEIR ANCESTORS TO GIVE THEM; AND YOU WILL PUT THEM IN POSSESSION OF IT. IT IS THE LORD WHO GOES BEFORE YOU. HE WILL BE WITH YOU; HE WILL NOT FAIL YOU OR

FORSAKE YOU. DO NOT FEAR OR BE DISMAYED."
DEUTERONOMY 31:1-8 (NRSV)

Base of Mount Sinai, Sinai Peninsula, Egypt

I recently traveled from Jerusalem to Jericho to Mount Sinai, backtracking lands traveled during the Exodus. The Sinai Desert is mountainous, rocky, rugged, dry and barren, words inadequate to describe how harsh the conditions are. Everything is sharp and dry. As we drove across the rocky land, I re-read Exodus, trying to imagine what it would have been like to walk across that land, those rocks, in the heat during the day and the cold at night, wearing sandals, carrying all my belongings, day after day for forty years. Exodus says that after a few weeks people started grumbling about the difficulty of the journey and the lack of food and water (see Exodus 16:1).

Taking in the entirety of the conditions I saw, I would have been grumbling after the first few hours.

God heard their cries in Egypt. He sent Moses to deliver them from captivity and to form them into His people, and He chose to accomplish all this through the events now known as the Exodus. God is sovereign. He has all authority in heaven and on earth. He can do anything and everything. He heard their prayers and He responded. At times His response was direct and miraculous, as seen in the parting of the sea (see Exodus 14), and at other times He sent people to accomplish His holy will. While the path may have been difficult, God was with them every step of the way, responding to their prayers and fulfilling their needs.

At the end of the journey, they camped on the Jordan River preparing to cross into the Promised Land and Moses delivered His farewell address, a portion of which is the passage first set forth above. Moses urges his friends and us to think back to the ways God has demonstrated His presence and protection and love, and trust and know in our hearts that He will continue to be with us in the future.

Scripture urges us to "be strong and bold … because it is the Lord your God who goes with you; he will not fail or forsake you." God is with you. Do not fear, do not be dismayed, do not worry, because God is with you. What an amazing promise!

Lyman Hardy designed, built and maintains a world-renowned water skiing lake just off Highway 82 in the hills southeast of Duncanville, Alabama. Serious competitors from across the US travel to the lakes, known as Lymanland, to train and compete.

Since the lake was built, Dr. Jim and Annette Mills have been regulars at Lymanland. Jim began competitive water skiing in high school and continued to train and compete at the lake into his 60's. On most weekends, Jim and his wife, Annette, enjoyed the lake together – Jim skied while Annette piloted the boat.

Skiing competitors recognize falls and injury are unfortunate risks of the sport – as they push the limits falls are inevitable and injury is a frequent side effect. Over the years, as he pursued his dream of winning nationals, Jim experienced countless spills on the lake. Sixteen years ago, after Jim fractured his femur during a fall, it took the ambulance about 45 minutes to arrive because of the lake's remote location.

On August 24, 2015, Annette was not able to go with him, so he went alone and met two others at the lake. Jim normally went to the lake without a cell phone because coverage at the remote location is intermittent, and on this particular day none of the three present had a cell phone.

While performing a specialized training maneuver, Jim was seriously injured. As his friends floated him to the nearest shore, Jim prayed aloud with them. When they reached the shore, their friend Lyman just happened to drive up in his pickup, he just happened to have his cell phone and, amazingly, it located a signal. He called 9-1-1 first, and Annette next. Her immediate reaction was to pray.

Over the course of the year to come, God revealed His glory time and time again in many ways, including this – He continuously placed the right person in their path at the right time. Time and time again it just so happened that the perfect person appeared offering the help that was needed.

The workers at the 9-1-1 call center located an ambulance that just happened be leaving the scene of a previous call about a mile from the lake, so an ambulance with trauma paramedics arrived at the lake within minutes of Lyman's call. The paramedics reviewed Jim's injuries, called the hospital and Dr. Simpson was waiting to see Jim as soon as he arrived. After a quick review, Dr. Simpson recommended that Jim transfer to UAB Hospital in Birmingham. It just happened that a helicopter had landed a few minutes earlier, delivering another patient, so it was on the helipad with engines running, blades turning and a flight crew on board ready to go. So Jim traveled from Lymanland to UAB Hospital in incredibly fast time, as if each segment of the relay was perfectly staged.

When he arrived at UAB, it just so happened that one of the best trauma surgeons and one of the leading orthopedic surgeons were both at the hospital, and both just happened to have empty schedules, so they were both able to help Jim immediately upon his arrival. By the time Annette arrived, Jim was in the surgical room. One of the surgeons met her in the waiting room. With x-rays in hand, he explained the ugly reality of Jim's condition, said that Jim's chance of survival was extremely low, and invited Annette into the surgical room to see Jim, suggesting it could very well be her last opportunity to see him alive. Annette explained to the doctors, nurses and everyone within hearing distance that God is mighty and powerful, He is in control and she would not listen to their negative talk because God was saving Jim.

But Jim had lost a lot of blood, his body was a torn mess, he was filled with bacteria-laden lake water, and the doctors discussed the chaos of all the immediate life-threatening concerns and worked to develop a plan. They needed wisdom. They needed discernment. The ICU nurses just happened to be prayer warriors. Annette and the ICU nurses prayed, filling the room with prayer revealing God's divine presence.

Time and time again God placed the right people in Jim and Annette's path. As the events unfolded that afternoon, word of Jim's injury spread and people started praying. One person described it as a "tsunami of prayer." Prayer filled our church and many churches and homes across the US and Honduras. God responded and with every step along Jim's amazingly speedy recovery, God placed the right person in his path at the right time.

Annette recalls two particularly meaningful verses. Deuteronomy 31:6 – "Do not be afraid or terrified because of them, for the Lord your God goes with you; he will never leave you nor forsake you" (see also Hebrews 13:5); and Philippians 4:9 – "Whatever you have learned or received or heard from me, or seen in me – put it into practice. And the God of peace will be with you." God and His peace were with Annette. He guarded her. He never allowed the thought of Jim dying into her mind. He protected her, comforted her and filled her with peace.

God revealed His glory in countless miraculous ways. Jim is tangible evidence of God's holy healing hand. As he describes it all, the entire story of God orchestrating events and healing and comforting and revealing His presence, Jim emphatically insists that the most amazing thing God has done in and for his life has been Annette, who in Jim's words is "the best nurse I've EVER had!"

THOUGHTS TO CONSIDER

1. Read Hebrews 13:1-6. In what specific ways do you know that God is with you?

2. Read Philippians 4:8-9. Do you believe, really believe in your heart, that God is with you?

3. Read Exodus 2. Moses was a murderer running from the law. Why did God choose Him?

4. Read Exodus 3:1-12. God revealed Himself to Moses through the miraculous display of a bush that burned but was not consumed, and He called Moses to serve Him by delivering His people out of bondage

in Egypt. God is sovereign. He has all power and authority. He created everything by speaking. He breathes life into each of us. Why didn't He simply snap His spiritual fingers and cause Pharaoh to set His people free?

5. For reasons we may not understand, God often chooses to work through people whom He calls into His service. As you go through your life today, consider who He is placing in your path to deliver you in your time of need, to shine His light on your darkness.

6. Pray. And as you do, ask God to open your ears to hear His call, to open your eyes to see the opportunities in your path today to serve Him, to be His beacon of light, to help Him as He calls you to serve as His agent of deliverance, and to give you His courage and power and strength to act. What did you hear and see in response to your prayer?

2

BELIEVE, SEEK & SEE

AND WITHOUT FAITH IT IS IMPOSSIBLE TO PLEASE GOD, FOR WHOEVER WOULD APPROACH HIM MUST BELIEVE THAT HE EXISTS AND THAT HE REWARDS THOSE WHO SEEK HIM. HEBREWS 11:6 (NRSV)

THEN JESUS, AGAIN GREATLY DISTURBED, CAME TO THE TOMB. IT WAS A CAVE, AND A STONE WAS LYING AGAINST IT. JESUS SAID, "TAKE AWAY THE STONE." MARTHA, THE SISTER OF THE DEAD MAN, SAID TO HIM, "LORD, ALREADY THERE IS A STENCH BECAUSE HE HAS BEEN DEAD FOUR DAYS." JESUS SAID TO HER, "DID I NOT TELL YOU THAT IF YOU BELIEVED, YOU WOULD SEE THE GLORY OF GOD?" SO THEY TOOK AWAY THE STONE. AND JESUS LOOKED UPWARD AND SAID, "FATHER, I THANK YOU FOR HAVING HEARD ME. I KNEW THAT YOU ALWAYS HEAR ME, BUT I HAVE SAID THIS FOR THE SAKE OF THE CROWD STANDING HERE, SO THAT THEY MAY BELIEVE THAT YOU SENT ME." WHEN HE HAD SAID THIS, HE CRIED WITH A LOUD VOICE, "LAZARUS, COME OUT!" THE DEAD MAN CAME OUT, HIS HANDS AND FEET BOUND WITH STRIPS OF CLOTH, AND HIS FACE WRAPPED IN A CLOTH. JESUS SAID TO THEM, "UNBIND HIM, AND LET HIM GO." JOHN 11:38-44 (NRSV)

Mount of Olives, Jerusalem, Israel

Our ability to see God's glory revealed around us is connected to our belief. Do you believe God exists? Do you believe He reveals His glory through His creation?

Martha and Mary believed Jesus could heal their brother. They sent Him a message that Lazarus was sick, they believed that He would have healed their brother had He been there in time, but they never imagined Jesus was the Author of life with power over life and death. They believed, but their belief was limited.

Jesus waited until the perfect time to reveal God's glory. He waited until there could be no doubt that Lazarus had really died, and God really returned him to life. He says, "Did I not tell you that if you believed, you would see the glory of God?"

Some present saw the events, they saw Lazarus walk out of the tomb wrapped in burial cloth, yet they did not believe, they did not see God's holy hand at work in the events. Do you believe? Jesus is God. He has always been and always will be. He has all authority in heaven and earth. He is sovereign. There is nothing he cannot do, and He knows everything. He knows our needs better than we do. He is love. He loves us. He loves you. He was also fully human, sharing our human experience. Do you believe all that?

It is one thing to accept the words intellectually, and an entirely different thing to accept intimately, in the depths of our spirit, the life changing reality they represent. Through Jesus the miraculous is always possible. He often reaches into our realm to influence events in response to prayer. He does so to reveal God's glory, and to provide tangible assurance of His presence and tangible affirmation of our faith, but we must have eyes to see, ears to hear, faith to ask, and a relationship with Him. Sometimes He touches directly in a huge, medically verified, life-changing way where the most logical explanation is Jesus healed through His miraculous touch, exactly like miracles recorded in Scripture. Other times, the tangible result of His touch is subtle.

With all the things going on in our family over the past decade, we have experienced a lot of opportunities to see God's glory. A few years ago we traveled to Texas under horrific circumstances. To keep this brief, I will not get into the details, but our son's freedom hung in the balance and it was extremely stressful. Lori and I left early to catch a flight, rushed from meeting to meeting, and after a long stressful day, we went to a hotel.

We were physically and emotionally exhausted. We needed to eat, but neither of us had an appetite and none of the available options sounded good. Lori went to bed, but she could not sleep. Her skin turned red and itchy and bumps started forming, and she could find no comfort. She thought she was allergic to the laundry detergent on the sheets. I did not say anything, but I thought it was the cumulative effect of stress and lack of sleep and lack of good food and the travel and the general chaos that was our life at that particular moment.

I remembered a couple things I had read years earlier in two different books. I do not recall who wrote either, but I recalled a woman writing that we often pray for God change the world yet we lack the faith to ask Him to cure our common cold. And I recalled a father describe a late night when his young son had an earache and would not stop crying. The father prayed and his son immediately stopped crying, slept peacefully and the next day doctors found no evidence of problem.

So I put my hand on Lori's shoulder and said the simplest prayer. I asked God to give her sleep and to take away her skin problems. Within a few minutes she fell asleep and when she awoke her skin was fine.

I know. It was not a sight-restoring miracle or Lazarus returning to life and the chaos of the world continued to swirl around us, but at that moment He gave us what we needed. He provided for our physical needs and He provided assurance of His holy presence. He reminded us that He never leaves us, that His love never fades, and that He knows what we are going through. He heard that simple prayer and He responded.

If you believe you will see God's glory revealed. God rewards those who seek Him. May you seek Him, may He enlighten the eyes of your spirit, may you receive His peace and comfort, and may He continue to reveal His glory to you and through you.

THOUGHTS TO CONSIDER

1. Do you struggle to believe that God reaches into our world and acts in response to our prayers?

2. Martha and Mary believed, but their belief was limited. They believed that had Jesus been physically present while Lazarus lived He would have healed Lazarus, but they failed to believe that Jesus could raise their brother back to life. In what ways does your belief attempt to limit God?

3. When was the last time you asked God to cure your common cold, or help you sleep? What happened in response to your prayer?

4. Read John 20:24-27. In what ways are you like Thomas?

3

SEEK FIRST

SO DO NOT WORRY, SAYING, 'WHAT SHALL WE EAT?' OR 'WHAT SHALL WE DRINK?' OR 'WHAT SHALL WE WEAR?' FOR THE PAGANS RUN AFTER ALL THESE THINGS, AND YOUR HEAVENLY FATHER KNOWS THAT YOU NEED THEM. BUT SEEK FIRST HIS KINGDOM AND HIS RIGHTEOUSNESS, AND ALL THESE THINGS WILL BE GIVEN TO YOU AS WELL. THEREFORE DO NOT WORRY ABOUT TOMORROW, FOR TOMORROW WILL WORRY ABOUT ITSELF. EACH DAY HAS ENOUGH TROUBLE OF ITS OWN. MATTHEW 6:31-34

We gather together each week in the Sanctuary to pray. We begin by discussing prayer concerns, singing hymns, worshiping God, praising Him, enjoying Holy Communion, and then we pray. We seek Him and enter into holy fellowship with Him and offer our thanks and praise. We continue praying with and for others.

Recently, as we prayed over each card from the congregation requesting prayer, I wept over the heart wrenching requests and the people making them. Prayer is requested for health concerns, loved ones, relationships, guidance for significant decisions, pets, personal spiritual transformation, and other topics. A woman prays for her family as they proceed through divorce. A child prays for her lost cat. Another child prays for her father. A man prays for a job. There are so many prayers regarding life-threatening health concerns – people struggling with cancer, preparing for surgery, suffering with long-term illness, etc.

We do not know who wrote each card, but God knows. We do not fully understand their needs, but God knows. He knows each of us better than we know ourselves, He understands our needs, He is almighty God, He is Creator of all things. Nothing is beyond His authority or power or reach, He loves each of us, we know He hears our prayers, and we trust He responds.

God encourages us to bring all our concerns and needs to Him with open, honest transparency. Scripture urges us to pray all the time (see 1 Thessalonians 5:17). Jesus urges us to pray persistently and with "shameless audacity" (Luke 11:8), and in His next breath, Jesus instructs us to ask, seek and knock (see Luke 11:9-10). We should reach out to God with all your concerns. We should ask God to help with physical needs and spiritual needs. We should bare our souls to Him without ceasing.

But asking for help is not the first step. In the Sermon on the Mount, Jesus tells us the first step is seeking Him. "Seek first his kingdom and his righteousness, and all these things will be given to you as well" (Matthew 6:33). Actively pursue Him. Hunt Him down. Chase Him with all your energy and focus.

As you begin this endeavor, please realize two things. First, seeking Him is a process that will continue the rest of your life. It is a journey. It is daily pursuit towards Jesus Christ, towards the kingdom of God, towards holiness. Jesus urges us to "Be perfect, therefore, as your heavenly Father is perfect" (Matthew 5:48). Similarly, Peter urges us to be holy (see 1 Peter 1:15). We may never achieve perfection or holiness, but we can inch along the path little by little, step by step, day by day. We simply need to keep moving in the right direction. And as we seek Him, we reach out to Him in prayer and ask for His help, thus the asking, seeking and knocking become blended.

Second, it involves surrender. As we encounter Him, we must relinquish our need to control everything, we must let go of worldly pursuits separating us from Him, and we must allow Him to transform our spirits and souls through His indwelling holiness. We must surrender our worry and replace it with trust.

Our lives are better when lived in communion with Jesus Christ. Please continue reaching out to God with all your concerns and needs. And as you wake each morning, as you go through your day, as you go to bed at night, I urge you to seek Him first and trust in His promises.

Basilica de la Sagrada Familia, Barcelona, Catalonia, Spain

THOUGHTS TO CONSIDER

1. Read Matthew 5:43-48. In the Sermon on the Mount, Jesus urges us to love our enemies and to pray for the people who persecute us. He mentions the way that everyone treats people who are kind to them with kindness, and contrasts that with the way God sends blessings to people who are righteous and also to people who are not righteous. God loves everyone, and Jesus urges us to love everyone in the same way. With this in mind, He urges us to be perfect "as your heavenly Father is perfect" (Matthew 5:48). In what tangible ways does seeking God help you grow towards perfection?

2. Read 1 Peter 1:13-15 and Leviticus 19:1-4. In his first epistle, Peter quotes Leviticus and urges us to be holy as God is holy. Describe what holiness looks like and ways you try to achieve holiness.

3. Read 1 Thessalonians 5:12-28. In his final exhortation in his first epistle written to the church in Thessalonica, Paul urges us to maintain healthy relationships with one another (to love one another, to live peaceably with one another, and to encourage and help one another), and to maintain a healthy relationship with God (rejoice in and worship God, give thanks to God, pray continuously, welcome the Holy Spirit and abstain from evil). How does your relationship with God influence your relationships with other people?

4. Jesus urges us to seek God first. What tangible steps do you take each day to accomplish this?

Masada, Israel

4

PRAYING THE PSALMS

WHOEVER DWELLS IN THE SHELTER OF THE MOST HIGH WILL REST IN THE SHADOW OF THE ALMIGHTY... IF YOU SAY, "THE LORD IS MY REFUGE," AND YOU MAKE THE MOST HIGH YOUR DWELLING, NO HARM WILL OVERTAKE YOU, NO DISASTER WILL COME NEAR YOUR TENT. FOR HE WILL COMMAND HIS ANGELS CONCERNING YOU TO GUARD YOU IN ALL YOUR WAYS; THEY WILL LIFT YOU UP IN THEIR HANDS, SO THAT YOU WILL NOT STRIKE YOUR FOOT AGAINST A STONE. PSALM 91:1 & 9-12 (NRSV)

Saint Peter's Basilica, Vatican City

Freddie glows with God's glory shining through her. She was a child with dark skin living in Alabama during the 1960's call for civil rights, and she experienced many awful things that humans are capable of doing to one another. One Sunday morning when she was a young girl, she walked along a sidewalk in downtown Tuscaloosa, Alabama where well-dressed white church greeters ordered her to cross the street because she was not welcome on their side. Many years later while living in Maryland, she heard God's call. He asked her to return to Tuscaloosa to start a radio ministry, and she did, and her program reaches an untold number of listeners each week. Today she is a spiritual leader; faithfully serving the very church whose greeters once ordered her to cross the street.

When Freddie prays, windows open revealing the kingdom of heaven. I have been in her presence as we pray over people in need, and the energy and power and warmth of the Holy Spirit flows like electricity. She is truly a prayer warrior. During a prayer meeting she asked, "Have you considered praying the Psalms?" Many had not heard of the idea, so she explained what she meant. She read a passage from Psalms. Then she personalized the words, making the Psalm, God's holy word, her personal prayer.

Not long after the meeting, I read a note by Billy Graham in which he described reading five Psalms and one Proverb each day, progressing through both books each month. Shortly after that, I happened across an entry by a different author describing his practice of meditating daily on the Psalms. He continued explaining that the practice added depth and richness to his prayer life. These statements caught my attention because of Freddie's recent question, and I started reading Psalms with intention. I focused on God's promises and I converted the passages into my personal prayers in an effort to blend God's holy word, His truth, into my spirit and soul, welcoming His holy presence into my spirit in a new way.

My prayer life recedes and grows in a cycle punctuated by alternating episodes of distraction and focus. At times I feel dry and empty, lacking connection, searching for inspiration. When I feel like that, the Psalms have been a terrific source of life, energy and fuel for my spirit. Praise God for delivering thoughts through holy people to me.

A couple months after God encouraged me to see the Psalms with new eyes, I was in Houston for a series of meetings. One morning I woke way earlier than I needed to and I felt a strong need to read Psalm 91. I had no idea why, but I read it several times, and verses 9-12 jumped off the page to me. "If you say, 'The Lord is my refuge,' and you make the Most High your dwelling, no harm will overtake you... he will command his angels ... to guard you ... they will lift you up in their hands." So I prayed the Psalm focusing on verses 9-12. I thanked God for being my refuge and my dwelling. I praised God and thanked God for His promises, His protection, for sending His angels to protect us, for lifting us up. I praised and thanked God. As I prayed the alarm went off and I continued praying while I got ready for my first meeting and walked the downtown streets to it. I pondered seeking refuge in the Lord and dwelling in Him and abiding in Jesus Christ and He abiding in me. I pondered the vine and the branches and the fruit.

At about five minutes before 8, as I walked into the conference room, I felt my phone vibrating in my pocket. I pulled it out to see it was my son calling me. There are few calls that I would have taken in that moment, but when I saw it was my son, I excused myself, stepped back into the hallway and answered the phone.

He was calling to inform me that he had just been involved in a car accident. He said another car ran a stop sign and hit him. He was confident his car had been totaled. He said he was a little bruised but fine. He said, as he stood back and looked at his car, he was amazed that he survived the accident. He was miraculously okay.

Praise God. By nudging me awake and causing me to focus on His holy word, He gave me eyes to see His glorious protection unveiled through the accident. My son's car was a crumpled, mangled mess, but my son was virtually unharmed. God protected him and through the prayer, I could visualize His angels surrounding my son, protecting him as the car folded around him. He gave me eyes to see His holy hand at work.

And that knowledge affirms my faith. I know and trust that He continues to watch over us today. I know that He continues to send His angels to protect us. And as I pray, I thank God for His holy healing hand, for the healing He has done, is doing and will accomplish in the future, for his protection, for His angels, for His Son, for His Holy Spirit and for all His blessings.

Praise God. May we each have eyes to see, ears to hear and hearts to receive His love.

Thoughts to Consider

1. Read Psalm 91. Convert the Psalm into your personal prayer.

2. In what specific ways is God your refuge?

3. Read John 15:1-17. Over and over in His teaching about the vine and the branches, Jesus urges us to abide, dwell, remain in Him. Jesus calls us to "Abide in [him] as [he abides] in us" (v.15:4, NRSV). How do you accomplish this?

4. Think about your experiences. Describe specific times when God has sent His angels to protect you, "to lift you up in their hands..."

Western Wall of the Second Jewish Temple, Jerusalem, Israel

5

GOD'S PROTECTION

SO DO NOT WORRY, SAYING, 'WHAT SHALL WE EAT?' OR 'WHAT SHALL WE DRINK?' OR 'WHAT SHALL WE WEAR?' FOR THE PAGANS RUN AFTER ALL THESE THINGS, AND YOUR HEAVENLY FATHER KNOWS THAT YOU NEED THEM. BUT SEEK FIRST HIS KINGDOM AND HIS RIGHTEOUSNESS, AND ALL THESE THINGS WILL BE GIVEN TO YOU AS WELL. THEREFORE DO NOT WORRY ABOUT TOMORROW, FOR TOMORROW WILL WORRY ABOUT ITSELF. EACH DAY HAS ENOUGH TROUBLE OF ITS OWN. MATTHEW 6:31-34

Can you tell this passage weighs heavy on my heart? It continues to haunt me in so many ways. As I pursue things am I acting like a pagan? Jesus commands me not to worry, but I worry. I may not worry about whether I will have food to eat today or whether I will have clothes to wear today, but I wonder whether I will be able to afford life at some undefined future time. Does this cause me to be less generous today than I should be? Does this create a miserly spirit within me when I should be loving, compassionate and generous?

Jesus addresses our worry. His words focus on physical needs, but as I read His words I think about other worries in my life. It is easy – it even feels natural – for me to worry about my family, my children's decisions, the evil surrounding us in the world, and the decisions I make each day charting our path forward. I pray for God's protection, for His guidance, for His direction, and for Him to enlighten my eyes to see, open my ears to hear and soften my heart to receive Him. I pray that He place a hedge of protection around my children, separating them from evil and removing any pleasure they might otherwise find from poor choices. I pray that we might each have hearts to receive His holy grace that continuously rains over us all.

I know God is present. I know He has all authority and power. I know He is sovereign. I know He created everything, He breathes the breath of life into each of us, and our efforts to create are simply manipulations of that which He already made. I know He can do anything and everything. I know He loves us, hears our prayers, and responds to our petitions. I know all this, but I still worry.

Worry is a symptom of deeper problems. It is a sign that I do not really trust God, and that my intellectual belief is not deeply rooted in my spiritual being. It represents a gap – I may possess the intellectual knowledge of everything God represents and offers, but I am somehow preventing that intellectual knowledge from transforming my core spiritual being.

I feel a bit like the father who asks Jesus to heal his son, and who then says, "I believe; but help my unbelief!" (Mark 9:24). As you consider that scene, notice Jesus' compassion and grace. In response to the father's declaration, his admission of unbelief, Jesus answers his prayer. The father seeks Jesus with open, honest, unveiled humility, and Jesus responds with loving compassion and grace.

As Jesus discusses worry, He offers the cure – "seek first his kingdom and his righteousness..." Seek Him. The short sentence implies an acknowledgment that we need Him, which means we realize, accept and declare our frailty. Jesus knows none of us are perfect. He knows we are each a work in progress. He accepts us where we are if we simply seek Him and reveal our unveiled hearts to Him. And He offers Himself to fill the void in our lives.

"So do not worry…" At first glance it sounds like a command, like a rule to follow. With further scrutiny, it is an offer, a promise. If we seek Him, He will replace our worry with His love, compassion and grace. Once we realize and truly accept that He has our back, worry becomes an unnecessary waste of time and energy. I pray that some day my intellectual knowledge of that principle permeates my spiritual being.

God's glory shines upon you. May you have eyes to see, ears to hear and a heart to experience His loving grace.

Jerusalem, Israel

Thoughts to Consider

1. Do you believe that God exists, that He is sovereign, that He has all authority in heaven and on earth, that He is all-powerful, that He loves you, that He hears your prayers, that He is true to His promises and that He promises to respond?

2. Make a list of the things that keep you awake at night. Which of those things is too big for God to handle?

3. Read Mark 9:14-29. Jesus, Peter, James and John had just shared the most amazing mountain top experience. They heard God speak to them audibly, with their ears, and suddenly Elijah and Moses joined them on the mountaintop, and Jesus' physical appearance changed – his clothes became whiter than possible on earth (see Mark 9:2-13). After that, they walked down the mountain. When they encountered the disciples with a crowd of people and they met a father with a demon-possessed boy. The disciples had tried to remove the evil spirit, but they failed and the father was desperate and in his desperation his belief faded into doubt. He cried out to Jesus, "I believe; but help my unbelief!" (Mark 9:24). When have you had similar experiences? When you cried out to Jesus for help, how did He respond?

4. Do you accept the notion that "do not worry" is a promise, not a command? Why or why not?

6

GOD HEALS KENNEDY

I LOVE YOU, O LORD, MY STRENGTH. THE LORD IS MY ROCK, MY FORTRESS, AND MY DELIVERER; MY GOD IS MY ROCK, IN WHOM I TAKE REFUGE. HE IS MY SHIELD AND THE HORN OF MY SALVATION, MY STRONGHOLD. I CALL TO THE LORD, WHO IS WORTHY OF PRAISE, AND I AM SAVED FROM MY ENEMIES. ... HE REACHED DOWN FROM ON HIGH AND TOOK HOLD OF ME; HE DREW ME OUT OF DEEP WATERS. HE RESCUED ME FROM MY POWERFUL ENEMY, FROM MY FOES WHO WERE TOO STRONG FOR ME. PSALM 18:1-3; 16-17

Our realm is a place of great contrast. God allows inconsistent, competing forces to exist. He allows free will and He allows evil to roam the earth. Our realm is also the place where He reveals His glory and acts in response to prayer to help us through times of trouble. He does not promise to immediately remove trouble or to immediately remove us from trouble, rather He promises to be with us in our trouble (see Psalm 91:15).

And so it is with many miracle stories. When Jesus raised Lazarus from the tomb, He allowed His close friend to suffer and die before revealing God's glory through the miraculous raising (see John 11). Certainly God could have prevented Lazarus from getting sick, certainly God could have healed Lazarus early in the illness, certainly He could have removed Lazarus' suffering, but God opted for the path that would maximize the revelation of His glory. As the events unfolded, God's glory has rippled through the generations each time the story is retold. But we must have eyes capable of seeing His glory.

I am reminded of God revealing His glory through Kennedy Buettner beginning on June 15, 2000 in Tuscaloosa, Alabama. Kennedy was four. After his ten-year-old brother played in a baseball game, the team and their families gathered at the home of one of the players for a pool party.

They swam before gathering to eat. Kennedy's mother, Amy, helped him and his four siblings get settled with food. Then she and Craig sat down to eat. Kennedy was sitting on a towel eating with some older boys. As she ate, Amy scanned the scene making sure her kids were okay and she suddenly realized Kennedy was missing. Kids were playing on bikes and riding toys. She was certain he was playing with them. She started walking around looking for him. As she looked she asked people if they had seen him. Soon everyone was looking for Kennedy.

Sea of Galilee near Tiberias, Israel

Kennedy's brother saw Kennedy lying at the bottom of the pool. They pulled him to the surface. His body was limp, bloated and grayish blue. His father, Craig, is a physician. He performed CPR. Someone called 9-1-1. Men and women gathered to pray. After about five minutes of CPR, Kennedy's heart began beating erratically.

An ambulance rushed Kennedy to the local hospital and a helicopter flew him to Children's Hospital in Birmingham. The medical diagnosis was clear. He was possibly underwater for ten minutes. Add that to five minutes of CPR and his brain had been without oxygen for as long as fifteen minutes. His chance of survival was slim, and if he survived, his brain would be severely damaged.

The Buettner family was bathed in prayer. Friends drove to meet them to pray with them in the hospital. Churches and individuals around the community prayed. Less than a week later, with tubes preventing him from speaking, Kennedy pointed to the television. He then held up four fingers, closed his fist, and held up four fingers again. He was requesting that the television be turned on to channel 44, the Cartoon Network. A week after the incident he returned home. He recovered fully.

While the story of his miraculous healing is wonderful, even more amazing is what he saw while his body slept. The four-year-old described flying with an angel who wore long white clothes. They flew through walls, through clouds, through his mother as she knelt over him praying, and to heaven. Kennedy said while in heaven he stood on glass and was invisible, and he described talking with Jesus. He described seeing a volcano with sad people and a dragon in it. He said he was not afraid.

While working to heal Kennedy's body, Jesus gave him a remarkable heavenly tour. And through it, God reveals His glory. Certainly God could have prevented Kennedy from entering the pool. God could have kept Kennedy afloat preventing the incident. God could have done so many things to prevent the situation, but had He done so, we would not be retelling the story. Through Kennedy and through many other remarkable situations, God reveals His glory.

May you have eyes to see, ears to hear and a heart to experience God's glory shining around you, and may you allow God's glory to flow through you.

Thoughts to Consider

1.   Read Revelation 21:15-27. Kennedy's description of heaven was consistent with John's heavenly vision recorded in Revelation.

2.   Read Psalm 91. What do you think about God's promise to be with us in our trouble? How have you experienced God's holy presence in your times of trouble?

3.   Read John 11. Does Kennedy's story cause you to believe that God continues to reach His holy, healing, miraculous touch into our realm today? Why or why not?

4.   If you would like to read more about Kennedy's amazing story, his parents have written about the experience.   The information provided above is adapted from their writing.   For more information, please see the following:

> Buettner, Amy, "Mommy, I Saw Jesus," Christianity Today International / Today's Christian Magazine, November/December 2002, Vol. 40, No. 6, p.68, (2002).

Buettner, Dr. Craig and Buckstreet, J.C. <u>Kennedy: A Story of God's Grace,</u> (March 25, 2014, Amazon Digital Services).

Basilica de la Sagrada Familia, Barcelona, Catalonia, Spain

7

REVELATION THROUGH THE ORDINARY

THE HEAVENS DECLARE THE GLORY OF GOD; THE
SKIES PROCLAIM THE WORK OF HIS HANDS. PSALM 19:1

Last night I saw the most amazing sunset. As the sun neared the horizon, two large clouds hovered high in the sky. The lower one was a blended spectrum of lavender, from dark shades to light hues. The cloud above it revealed bright pink, peach, orange, yellow, cream and blends of them all that I cannot describe. Its western edge highlighted wisps of bright yellowy white. As I watched, the higher cloud moved slightly to the east revealing an incredible crescent moon. I looked to the darkened eastern sky and saw a cloud illuminated by distant lightning strikes. I stood in the yard taking it all in. God brought His art gallery to me.

God is the creator and He acts through His creation. Where do you see His holy hand at work?

As we read Exodus, we understand that the former slaves saw God's hand at work in their daily lives. They saw God's provision as they collected manna, captured quail, carried water and cooked their meals. They saw God's provision for them throughout each day, even though they had to work to obtain the gifts. Is the food you eat today, the air you currently breathe, the water you drink a gift from God? Is your occupation a gift from God providing not only daily sustenance, but also opportunities to serve Him?

I have been reading a fascinating book on the history of the Old Testament. The authors provide a scientific explanation for manna, saying that certain desert insects eat tamarisk twigs and excrete a sticky substance that accumulates overnight.[i] I am not sure whether the explanation is scientifically accurate, but assuming it is, does it influence your thinking?

Does the scientific explanation cause you to see God's fingerprints more clearly on the gift of manna, does it cause you to wonder whether God really provided the manna, or does it have no influence on your view? For some, science enhances their view of God's hand at work. They see His holy fingerprints in the precision of order, and the intricacy of design and function. Others desire to see God purely through miraculous, supernatural events defying scientific explanation and expectation. Of course, some fail to see God at all.

Do you see God's hand at work? If so, do you see Him in ordinary events following the natural order of things, in the miraculous where the laws of nature are suspended, or both? I know the beautiful colors in the clouds are the result of suspended water vapor creating shadows and reflecting and refracting light from the Sun. I also know the vapor, the sunlight, and the interaction between them are part of God's creation, and I see God's holy hand at work through the glorious scene in the sky.

God is the creator and He acts through His creation. He acts through you and me, and He paints with water vapor and sunlight in the sky. The former slaves of the Exodus saw God's hand in their daily life because they had eyes to see Him and His work. Where do you see His holy hand at work? May you have eyes to see God's hand at work in the world around you, and when you do, praise God!

Sinai Desert, Egypt

THOUGHTS TO CONSIDER

1.   Read Psalm 19. Do you hear the heavens silently proclaim God's glory? Does God's holy word revive your soul? Does His command enlighten your eyes? Do you desire God more than riches and more than personal pleasure?

2.   Read Exodus 16. In the evening quail covered the camp. In the morning, when the dew lifted, manna covered the land. God provided quail and manna, but the people still had to work six days each week: they had to capture quail, gather manna, and prepare and cook them. Do you see parallels to your daily routine?

3.   Does your understanding of science illuminate or hinder your view of God's holy hand at work in the world around us? Why?

Cattedrale di Santa Maria del Fiore, Florence, Italy

8

GOD WORKS THROUGH PEOPLE

"SO NOW, GO. I AM SENDING YOU TO PHARAOH TO BRING MY PEOPLE THE ISRAELITES OUT OF EGYPT." EXODUS 3:10

THE LORD TURNED TO HIM AND SAID, "GO IN THE STRENGTH YOU HAVE AND SAVE ISRAEL OUT OF MIDIAN'S HAND. AM I NOT SENDING YOU?" JUDGES 6:14

Saint Peter's Square, Vatican City

God often uses ordinary people to help Him perform extraordinary feats. For reasons I do not understand, God desires to work through regular folks like you and me. I think of the awful things I have done that should disqualify me from serving the holy One, but He calls nonetheless. If we allow Him, He will use the broken, tarnished vessels that we are in His glorious service, and when He calls, He calls us to go out in the world and act on His behalf.

Scripture provides many accounts of God's call. In the first passage above God calls Moses. In the second, God enlists Gideon. In each, God knew the person was capable of doing far more than they imagined. Before experiencing God's call, neither envisioned himself doing great things, but through God these ordinary people accomplished extraordinary feats.

Moses was a fugitive from justice – he murdered an Egyptian guard, fled east, and sought refuge with a Midianite priest who took him in. One day while tending the Midianite's flock, Moses met God through a bush that burned but was not consumed by the flame. Moses stood on sacred ground and engaged in conversation with God, all while watching the miracle of the bush, yet he still did not believe that he was capable of performing the task that God called him to do. So God promised to help Moses every step of the way saying, "Now go; I will help you speak and will teach you what to say" (Exodus 4:12).

Twice in the conversation God said, "Now go." Ultimately, Moses followed God's call. He went. He led the Israelites out of Egypt, through the wilderness and to the Promised Land. Along the way his faith was tested and he grew to become a pillar of faith.

About 300 years later, Gideon lived in the Promised Land, but Midianites who controlled the region oppressed Israelites and ravaged the land. While many fled to fortified caves and cliffs in the mountains, others assimilated into local society and worshiped local gods. Gideon was hiding out in a winepress threshing wheat when an angel appeared and called him "mighty warrior" (Judges 6:12). He did not believe the angel's words and objected to the "mighty warrior" designation saying that he was the lowest person in the weakest clan (Judges 6:15).

Ultimately Gideon also followed God's call and God did amazing things through him, but the task required remarkable faith. God called Gideon to lead an army against the Midian forces. This alone would have required great faith, but God raised the stakes – He told Gideon to reduce his army from 32,000 to 300 men to ensure that everyone would know that God delivered the Israelites, and that the army did not do it on its own. When God reaches into our world and works, He wants us to have eyes open to see His glory revealed, even when He works through people.

When God called, neither Moses nor Gideon felt prepared to serve God. But by stepping out in faith, trusting God and allowing God to work through them, they each accomplished extraordinary feats.

You might be wondering, "So what?" What do these stories mean for me today? God calls ordinary people into His service. Moses was a murderer on the run from justice. Gideon was a man hiding out, laying low, and trying to avoid detection by his oppressors. Scripture does not mention that they were righteous, Godly or anything like that, which leads me to believe they were ordinary people who became extraordinary when they heard God's call and stepped out serving Him. And the task they were each called to do involved great risk. God called Moses to speak with Pharaoh, the most powerful man in the world at the time, and politely ask him to free his slaves. God called Gideon to attack an army so vast it could not be counted, and to do so with 300 men. God called them to assume great risk and to trust that God was truly with them, and when they did, they became extraordinary. God uses ordinary people to accomplish extraordinary feats, and God calls each of us into His holy service. He did it back then and He continues to do it today.

Please know that God is calling you. May you have eyes to see, ears to hear, a heart that is fertile soil for His holy seed to grow, and when you experience His call, may He infuse you with His courage, power, strength and protection as you carry out His extraordinary service. Grow from ordinary to extraordinary by allowing God to work through you.

THOUGHTS TO CONSIDER

1. Read Exodus 3 & 4. How did God respond when Moses expressed doubt? In what ways did God offer His assurance to Moses?

2. Read Judges 6. How did God respond when Gideon accused Him of abandoning His people? In what ways did God offer His assurances to Gideon?

3. In each passage, how did God respond to people who cried to Him for help?

4. List parallels between Moses, Gideon and God's call of each. If God's holy word reflects His desire to reveal Himself and His character to us, how should we expect God to call us?

5. Read Judges 6:36-40. Gideon heard God's call, but he nonetheless devised a test using fleece. Please do not interpret this as God instructing us to test Him when we hear His call. It is not. Gideon should have trusted God's call without needing to

test it. Please read this as another statement of God's mercy and grace and love, and His continued desire to use mere mortals as His agents out in the world.

6. Read John 20:24-29. How did Jesus respond when Thomas demanded proof that He had really risen? Jesus responded with mercy and grace and love, but He also rebuked Thomas saying, "Because you have seen me, you have believed; blessed are those who have not seen and yet have believed" (John 20:29).

Basilica de la Sagrada Familia, Barcelona, Catalonia, Spain

9

SEPARATE YET BLENDED

"YOU ARE SALT OF THE EARTH. BUT IF SALT LOSES ITS SALTINESS, HOW CAN IT BE MADE SALTY AGAIN? IT IS NO LONGER GOOD FOR ANYTHING, EXCEPT TO BE THROWN OUT AND TRAMPLED UNDERFOOT. YOU ARE LIGHT OF THE WORLD. A TOWN BUILT ON A HILL CANNOT BE HIDDEN. NEITHER DO PEOPLE LIGHT A LAMP AND PUT IT UNDER A BOWL. INSTEAD THEY PUT IT ON ITS STAND, AND IT GIVES LIGHT TO EVERYONE IN THE HOUSE. IN THE SAME WAY, LET YOUR LIGHT SHINE BEFORE OTHERS, THAT THEY MAY SEE YOUR GOOD DEEDS AND GLORIFY YOUR FATHER IN HEAVEN." MATTHEW 5:13-16

How do you separate yourself for our Lord? As you go about your life each day, what causes others to know that you follow Him? What is it about your life that distinguishes you from people who do not follow our Lord?

A few years ago I happened to schedule meetings in Chicago on Ash Wednesday. It was an icy grey day. Snow fell horizontally in the wind. As I entered my first meeting, I noticed a black blob on the receptionist's forehead. It took me a moment to remember the day was Ash Wednesday, to realize the blob was once a cross, and that the designation represented her faith in Jesus Christ. After I connected the dots, I saw her through different eyes. I suddenly saw her, not merely as the receptionist who would soon usher me to a conference room, but as a daughter of Christ and our brief interaction softened.

That evening as I walked the icy sidewalk to the hotel, I noticed lots and lots of people with black crosses on their foreheads fashioned from ash. At one stoplight, as I stood in a crowd waiting to cross, I looked at the people around me and while many foreheads were covered with hats, hoods or scarves, most of the uncovered foreheads bore an ashen cross. We crossed the street and I noticed crosses on most of the foreheads passing me, and as I stepped forward, block after block, the trend continued. People who not only followed Christ, but who took the time to attend church that day and refused to wipe the ashes from their skin surrounded me. They chose to bear the mark of the cross and to reveal that distinguishing mark to the world. Their simple act of faith, and possibly defiance to a cynical world, changed my view of the place and the people I encountered there, and it warmed that icy day.

Had I seen the same people at the same place on any other day, I would not have seen distinguishing marks and I may have overlooked evidence of their faith. How do we separate ourselves for our Lord and how do we reveal that separation to people around us?

Jesus explains that people who follow Him are different from the world around them – separated by holiness, yet sent into the world to be distinguished by good deeds (see John 17:13-19 and Matthew 5:16). It is one of the many terrific contradictions in Scripture. Jesus prays for us to be sanctified – to be made holy through the indwelling Truth. Yet in the same breath, He declares that He sends us into the world. We are to be separated by holiness yet blended into the world in such a way that the world is transformed and God's glory is revealed as a result of our presence.

He does not *call us to be* salt and light, He explains that *we are salt and light.* You *are* salt – you are the unique holy ingredient mixing in the world around you and transforming everything you contact with your unique, holy flavor. You *are* light shining in a dark world. As you allow God's love to flow through you, your good deeds shine His light and reveal His glory to the world. We separate ourselves through holiness, and continue to work in the world so that, through our loving action, God's glory becomes evident to people around us.

May God's love fill you, transform you, and flow through you, revealing His glory to the world.

THOUGHTS TO CONSIDER

1. Read John 17:13-19. John 17 records one of Jesus' prayers. After the Last Supper, before walking to the Garden of Gethsemane, Jesus prayed for Himself, for believers and for people who will come to believe through the believers. Jesus expresses His desire that believers will experience joy to the fullest; yet He acknowledges that the world will hate them because of their belief. Jesus asks God to protect believers from the evil one, and to sanctify them by God's truth.

2. To sanctify means to be set apart as holy. So the world will hate us because of our association with Christ, God desires to sanctify us, to set us apart as holy; yet Jesus calls us into the world as His salt and light. How do you reconcile these thoughts in your mind?

Possible location of Jesus' post-resurrection breakfast with the disciples
Tabgha, Israel

3. Read John 13:12-17. Jesus washed the disciples' feet, then says, "I have set you an example that you should do as I have done for you" (John 13:15). How does this teaching influence your understanding of what it means to be salt and light?

4. Read John 21:15-19.   Post-resurrection Jesus joined the disciples on the shore of the Sea of Galilee. He helped them catch an amazing mass of fish, He cooked breakfast for them, and as they ate, Jesus asked Peter to demonstrate his love for Jesus by serving other people.   Considering the totality of Scripture, I see it less as a demonstration of our love and more as a demonstration of Jesus Christ's love flowing through us. We are not the possessors of the love, rather the vessels through which it flows. How does this influence your understanding of what it means to be salt and light?

Saint Jerome's Grotto, Bethlehem, West Bank

10

Mercy Not Sacrifice

For I desire mercy, not sacrifice, and acknowledgment of God rather than burnt offerings. Hosea 6:6

Matthew records Jesus quoting this passage from Hosea on two occasions. As Jesus reclined in the tax collector's home eating with people deemed by many to be outcasts, religious leaders, shocked by His behavior, asked why Jesus broke bread with people like that. At another time Jesus walked through a wheat field on the Sabbath, picking heads of grain and eating them as He walked. Religious leaders accused Him of breaking the law of the Sabbath. On each occasion Jesus replied that the religious leaders should learn what the words mean, "I desire mercy, not sacrifice" (see Matthew 9:9-13 & 12:1-8).

We each view the world through our own perspective, crafted by all the influences of our lives. Religious leaders saw Jesus violating rules of ritual and worship. By eating with unclean people, Jesus defiled Himself and made Himself unworthy of worshiping God. By picking wheat on the Sabbath, Jesus defiled the day set aside for holiness and worship. Jesus had a different perspective. He saw that the leaders applied the rules in a way contradicting their original purpose, and He explains that mercy is a higher form of worship.

Do you see the connection? Loving God and loving our neighbor are the two most important commandments (see Matthew 22:37-40). One of the ways we worship God is by showing other people mercy and treating others with love and compassion. And if we fail to treat other people with love, all our other acts of worship – our attendance at church, our participation in Holy Communion, our tithes, our Bible study, our prayers, our good works – are hollow. By connecting our love for God with our love for one another, theology morphs into social responsibility.

As we read the interaction between Jesus and religious leaders, we might have the impression that Jesus introduces entirely new concepts. But the directive to care for people in need is woven throughout Scripture. During the Exodus, as God communicated the law through Moses, He explained rules relating to the tabernacle, offerings, sacrifices, festivals and worship, and blended the theme of caring for other people into the discussion. Time and time again in the books now known as Exodus, Leviticus and Deuteronomy, God explains that we are to care for orphans, widows, foreigners and others in need.[ii]

Centuries later, God sent prophets to restate the message and remind listeners to love their neighbor and to care for the poor and needy. The books of the prophets paint an image of God's people getting the rituals of worship right – they offered sacrifices, respected the festivals, worshiped and prayed – but they failed to love the least among them.

Isaiah writes, "Stop doing wrong, learn to do right! Seek justice, encourage the oppressed. Defend the cause of the fatherless, plead the case of the widow" (Isaiah 1:16-17).

Ezekiel compares Israel to Sodom (recall from Genesis 19 that God destroyed Sodom because of its evil residents) saying,

> "As surely as I live, declares the Sovereign Lord, your sister Sodom and her daughters never did what you and your daughters have done. Now this was the sin of your sister Sodom: She and her daughters were arrogant, overfed and unconcerned; they did not help the poor and

needy. They were haughty and did detestable things before me. Therefore, I did away with them as you have seen. Samaria did not commit half the sins you did. You have done more detestable things than they...." Ezekiel 16:48-50

What did the people of Sodom do that was so evil? Why did Sodom deserve destruction? According to God speaking through Ezekiel, Sodom's greatest sin was failing to help the poor and the needy.

Amos quotes God saying, "I hate, despise your religious feasts; I cannot stand your assemblies. Even though you bring me burnt offerings and grain offerings, I will not accept them. Though you bring choice fellowship offerings, I will have no regard for them. Away with the noise of your songs! I will not listen to the music of your harps. But let justice roll on like a river, righteousness like a never-failing stream!" (Amos 5:21-24).

The listeners were apparently attending church, worshiping, singing songs of praise and making offerings. They got the rituals of worship right, yet God was not pleased with them. What were they missing? They failed to love their neighbor. They failed to show love, mercy and compassion to people around them.

What about us? Do the words of Isaiah, Ezekiel, Amos and other prophets hit the mark with us? What about Jesus' words? He reserved His harshest criticism for folks who maintained an outward appearance of holiness while failing to love other people. On one occasion He called them "blind guides" and "whitewashed tombs" (Matthew 23:16 & 27).

I have the benefit of the Law of Moses, the teaching of the prophets, all of Jesus' teaching in Scripture, everything described in the New Testament, and the Holy Spirit convicting me, yet I still get it wrong every day. I know the words, but the gap between knowledge and action continues.

God desires mercy, not sacrifice. As we continue to worship God through praise, worship, prayer, study and song, may we also worship God by treating the people we encounter with love, compassion and mercy. May God open our eyes to see opportunities surrounding us to serve Him, may He open our ears to hear His call, may He soften our hearts allowing His seed to fall on fertile soil.

THOUGHTS TO CONSIDER

1. Read Matthew 23. Jesus instructs His disciples and the crowds to submit themselves to humble service of one another, and He blasts religious leaders for seeking honor and prestige of position while neglecting people in need, and for being more concerned with presenting the proper outward appearance than with "the weightier matters of the law: justice, mercy and faith" (Matthew 23:23). Are we guilty of doing the same thing?

2. Why do you attend church? List the reasons. Where does worshiping God, communing with other believers, seeking God, desiring to hear His holy voice fall on your list?

3. Think about your day yesterday, what tangible action did you take that reveals God's mercy, compassion and love to other people? Who were they? Did you know them?

Olive tree believed by some to be 2,000 years old
Garden of Gethsemane, Mount of Olives, Jerusalem, Israel

11

MERCY NOT SACRIFICE – PART II

WITH WHAT SHALL I COME BEFORE THE LORD AND BOW DOWN BEFORE THE EXALTED GOD? SHALL I COME BEFORE HIM WITH BURNT OFFERINGS, WITH CALVES A YEAR OLD? WILL THE LORD BE PLEASED WITH THOUSANDS OF RAMS, WITH TEN THOUSAND RIVERS OF OLIVE OIL? SHALL I OFFER MY FIRSTBORN FOR MY TRANSGRESSION, THE FRUIT OF MY BODY FOR THE SIN OF MY SOUL? HE HAS SHOWN YOU, O MORTAL, WHAT IS GOOD. AND WHAT DOES THE LORD REQUIRE OF YOU? TO ACT JUSTLY AND TO LOVE MERCY AND TO WALK HUMBLY WITH YOUR GOD. MICAH 6:6-8

Jesus explains that loving God and loving our neighbor are the two most important commandments (see Matthew 22:37-40). After peeling the layers to the core we see that the two are inseparable – by loving God with all our heart, mind and soul, His love flows through us revealing mercy, love and compassion to others, and when we allow this we are worshiping God. Worship, mercy, love and compassion are interwoven.

The reverse is also true. If we fail to treat other people with mercy, love and compassion, all our other acts of worship – our attendance at church, our participation in Holy Communion, our tithes, our Bible study, our prayers, our good works – are hollow and our witness suffers. For example, if I lead a meaningful Bible study at church then go to lunch where I am rude to the waitress, my witness suffers.

This is nothing new. It exposes a tendency of our human hearts and teaching on this topic goes back to the Exodus. As Moses explained how to worship, he gave rules relating to the tabernacle, sacrifices, offerings, festivals, and cleanliness, and scattered throughout the teaching was instruction to care for widows, orphans, foreigners and others in need. When God's people failed to care for people in need, He sent prophets, like Samuel, Isaiah, Ezekiel, Amos, Hosea, Malachi and others, to remind them to do so and to remind them that God takes His commands seriously.

Through the prophet Samuel, God reveals that He is serious about His commands. Saul disobeys God and after doing so, as he prepares to offer the spoils of his disobedience to God as sacrificial offering, God says through Samuel,

> Does the Lord delight in burnt offerings and sacrifices as much as in obeying the voice of the Lord? To obey is better than sacrifice, and to heed is better than the fat of rams. For rebellion is like the sin of divination, and arrogance like the evil of idolatry. Because you have rejected the word of the Lord, he has rejected you as king. 1 Samuel 15:22-23

Later, God sends Jeremiah as His spokesperson to His people. Through Jeremiah, God says,

> If you really change your ways and your actions and deal with each other justly, if you do not oppress the alien, the fatherless or the widow and do not shed innocent blood in this place, and if you do not follow other gods to your own harm, then I will let you live in this place, in the land I gave your forefathers for ever and ever. But look, you are trusting in deceptive words that are worthless. Jeremiah 7:5-8

Through Solomon, God says, "To do what is right and just is more acceptable to the Lord than sacrifice. Haughty eyes and a proud heart, the lamp of the wicked, are sin!" (Proverbs 21:3-4).

Throughout the Old Testament, God sends messengers urging His people to hear His voice, to listen to His words and to treat others with compassion. He urges His people to act with mercy and justice and love.

Later God sends John the Baptist to prepare the way for the Messiah, and he preaches the same message. Crowds travel to the wilderness to hear John preach his message of repentance. The message convicts them and they asked, "What should we do then?" John answers, "Anyone who has two tunics should share with him who has none, and the one who has food should do the same" (Luke 3:10-11). He continues explaining that tax collectors should continue doing their job, but they should collect no more than required, and soldiers should continue doing their job, but they should not extort or accuse people falsely (see Luke 3:12-14). As he prepares hearts to receive the Messiah, John instructs people to repent and to care for people with less power, lower standing and fewer possessions. He urges them to treat one another with mercy, love and compassion while they continue serving in their occupations.

And today, God's holy word speaks to us, His people, His adopted children, the Body of Christ. John's instructions include (i) freely giving from our excess and (ii) refraining from abusing the power of our position. Mercy, love and compassion involve both action and restraint. While recent headlines have been filled with accusations of men abusing the power of their positions, the condition of the human heart leading to decisions like that is nothing new. I say that not to dismiss abusive behavior – quite the opposite – it should be a warning for us all. We are each capable of abusing the power of our position in our own way. By recognizing that we each have human hearts and we each possess the frailty of our human condition, we should see with greater clarity that we need God in our lives, we need to surrender to Him and allow His love to flow through us and transform us. We need to understand in our hearts that loving God and loving other people are inseparable commandments.

"And what does the Lord require of you? To act justly and to love mercy and to walk humbly with your God" (Micah 6:8).

Father, we praise your holy name. We seek you; we need you in our lives. Please fill us with your holy, transforming Presence that we might grow towards truly loving you and truly loving the people we encounter each day. In Jesus' name, Amen.

THOUGHTS TO CONSIDER

1. Can you imagine ways you might be abusing the power of your position?

2. As you go through each day, how often do you miss opportunities to help others in need by failing to see, being in to too big of a hurry to stop, or simply refusing to help?

3. Read Mark 12:28-34. A religious leader asked Jesus about the most important of all of God's commands. Jesus replied saying the most important is to love God and the next is to love our neighbor. The religious leader agreed and continued saying that loving God and loving our neighbor "is more important than all burnt offerings and sacrifices" (Mark 12:33). Jesus commended the man saying, "You are not far from the kingdom of God" (Mark

12:34). Do you see any application of this message to your life?

4. Do you ever find that you are so busy complying with the ritual of worship that you fail to follow the greatest two commandments? If so, describe the details.

5. Consider your most recent week. What opportunities arose where you might have acted in a tangible way to promote justice and to show mercy? How did you respond to the opportunities? If similar opportunities arise in the future, how will you respond?

Masada, Israel

12

GLORY THROUGH SUFFERING

JESUS WENT THROUGHOUT GALILEE, TEACHING IN THEIR SYNAGOGUES, PREACHING THE GOOD NEWS OF THE KINGDOM, AND HEALING EVERY DISEASE AND SICKNESS AMONG THE PEOPLE. NEWS ABOUT HIM SPREAD ALL OVER SYRIA AND PEOPLE BROUGHT TO HIM ALL WHO WERE ILL WITH VARIOUS DISEASES, THOSE SUFFERING SEVERE PAIN, THE DEMON-POSSESSED, THOSE HAVING SEIZURES, AND THE PARALYZED; AND HE HEALED THEM. LARGE CROWDS FROM GALILEE, THE DECAPOLIS, JERUSALEM, JUDEA AND THE REGION ACROSS THE JORDAN FOLLOWED HIM. MATTHEW 4:23-25

Jesus heals and God reveals His glory through amazing situations, but not everyone sees it. On occasion, as a conversation morphs to matters of faith and I describe my faith in God, I see puzzled expressions in response. It is as if my efforts to communicate my experience with God are, in their mind, equivalent to saying I saw a unicorn, the Loch Ness Monster or Sasquatch. I know God is real. He is really real, really with us, and He really answers our prayers, but I encounter people who are somehow unable to see His light.

Paul explains this in terms of spiritual attack saying, "The god of this age has blinded the minds of unbelievers, so that they cannot see the light of the gospel that displays the glory of Christ, who is the image of God" (2 Corinthians 4:4). By writing "god" with a small case "g," Paul refers to evil influences, spiritual attack and the resulting spiritual blindness.

But God shines His glory through His creation and He responds to prayer, and when we have eyes to see His glory our faith is affirmed and strengthened. For some, it is a glimpse of His glory that softens their hearts allowing seeds of faith to grow. I have no idea why God allowed cancer to grow in my wife Lori's leg, but I know with certainty that He healed her, He has been with her every step along the path of her recovery, and He has and continues to reveal His glory through her and the situations surrounding her.

One year ago today, Lori descended her lowest point. She endured radiation, surgery removing a small football from the back of her thigh, and chemotherapy. Each chemo treatment involved four days of continuous infusion that destroyed her, followed by shots designed to revive her body's defenses. After each treatment, her body continued to decline for about a week before gradually recovering in preparation for the next treatment.

Her third treatment ended on Thursday, one week before Thanksgiving, so her low point was expected to occur on Thanksgiving. We prayed that the low point would happen sooner because our kids were traveling to be with us for Thanksgiving. They were both planning to arrive Wednesday. With the benefit of hindsight, we should have been careful about what we prayed for.

Wednesday morning Lori felt really, really bad. She had extreme shortness of breath, racing heart, and exhaustion. She walked 25 feet from bed to sofa, lost her breath and needed several minutes to recover. We went to the clinic for blood tests to make sure she was not experiencing symptoms of serious problems. After drawing blood, a nurse checked her vital signs. She did not have a fever, but her heart rate was racing at 144 beats per minute, and the machine was unable to measure her blood pressure. The nurse pulled out equipment to measure her blood pressure manually, but she was unable to get a reading. She called a second nurse who was unable to get a reading. Lori was struggling to sit up in her chair, so the nurses found a wheelchair and helped her into it. They then wheeled her into an exam room where a third nurse tried unsuccessfully to measure her blood pressure.

The nurses were very concerned. They knew Adriamycin is very hard on hearts; she had an elevated heart rate; her blood pressure was too low to read; and she barely had enough energy to sit in a chair. She just wanted to lie down, but the nurses told her with surprising sternness not to lie down. The nurses left to consult with a doctor. As Lori and I sat alone in the exam room I said a very short, simple prayer. It was really a faint whisper. A nurse returned with the doctor's order: he sent us to the Emergency Room.

I pushed Lori's wheelchair through the maze of hospital corridors to the Emergency Room, went through the admission process and as we entered the Emergency Room my cell phone started vibrating. I looked and it was a call from one of Lori's prayer warrior friends, a member of her prayer group. She never calls me. I did not answer it, but after we settled in a room I texted her explaining why I had ignored her call. She asked if she could forward my note to her prayer group and I said yes. About fifteen minutes later a nurse came to check Lori's vital signs. She hooked up the blood pressure monitoring machine and it measured without problem. Her blood pressure was a little low, but in the normal range, and her heart rate had dropped tremendously.

It was a different machine managed by a different nurse in a different part of the hospital about 30 minutes later. Lori had not been given any medication in the intervening time. I cannot think of any other difference between the attempted measurement in the Emergency Room and the clinic, except that during the intervening time a number of people were praying, and that was the difference that mattered. Her blood pressure rose from a level too low to detect to the normal range.

During that hospital stay, over the course of the following week many other instances arose allowing God's glory to shine through her situation. Time and time again God revealed His glory.

To underscore the low point she reached, after she left the hospital, one of the nurses commented, "I thought we were losing you." A few days ago Lori and I talked about the events of that day. She says that she vaguely remembers it, that she was not really there, that as we wheeled her to the Emergency Room she was sort of floating outside her body, and that she was at peace with the thought that she was about to die.

But God raised her from the depths. Praise God. He is good. Like Psalm 91:15 says, "He will call on me and I will answer him; I will be with him in trouble, I will deliver him and honor him." Praise God. He is with us and He delivers us.

You might be wondering, if God answered our prayer about low blood pressure and miraculously caused it to rise, why did He not miraculously touch Lori's leg and cure her cancer? Of course I do not know the answer, but I believe He wants to use her illness for many small opportunities to reveal His glory. He promises to be with us in trouble and to ultimately deliver us. He does not promise to remove us from trouble before we experience it. Often it is through our troubling times that He reveals His glory and prepares us to be able to serve Him in new and unique ways.

Praise God. May we each have eyes to see His glory.

Corinth, Greece

THOUGHTS TO CONSIDER

1.   Read 2 Corinthians 4.

 a.   Verses 1-6 discuss our ministry and God's light shining out of our hearts. Do you see your life as a ministry? In what ways does God's holy light shine through you? As you consider your life as a ministry, should you make any tangible changes to your life to allow your ministry to flourish? What changes should you make?

 b.   Verses 7-12 describe our physical bodies as clay jars – ordinary, weak, fragile – yet God fills us with the treasure of His light, life and love. If you were writing this passage today, what analogy would you use?

c. Verse 13 says, "We also believe and there speak." We believe, but do we speak? Do you feel comfortable speaking about your faith to people outside your community of faith? If not, why is that?

d. "For our light and momentary troubles are achieving for us an eternal glory that far outweighs them all" (v.17). Consider the troubles you have faced in the past. With the benefit of hindsight, can you see how God revealed His glory through your season of trouble? List specific instances. With this in mind, how do you feel about the troubles you are currently facing?

2. Read Luke 4:31 – 5:26. Describe similarities among the accounts of Jesus healing people. What do the passage mean to you today?

13

RELEASING OUR CHILDREN TO GOD

WHEN THEY HAD SLAUGHTERED THE BULL, THEY BROUGHT THE BOY TO ELI, AND SHE SAID TO HIM, "AS SURELY AS YOU LIVE, MY LORD, I AM THE WOMAN WHO STOOD HERE BESIDE YOU PRAYING TO THE LORD. I PRAYED FOR THIS CHILD, AND THE LORD HAS GRANTED ME WHAT I ASKED OF HIM. SO NOW I GIVE HIM TO THE LORD. FOR HIS WHOLE LIFE HE WILL BE GIVEN OVER TO THE LORD." AND HE WORSHIPED THE LORD THERE. 1 SAMUEL 1:25-28

The Pieta by Michelangelo, Saint Peter's Basilica, Vatican City[iii]

Hannah pleaded with God. She prayed for God to bless her with a child, and after He did, she responded by dedicating her son to God. As soon as Samuel was old enough, Hannah handed him to God and God called Samuel to serve as a prophet. She was still his mother, but she knew if Samuel was going to serve God he needed to leave her nest and live with a Godly mentor.

As parents, God blesses us with children. He calls us to raise them in His way and at the appropriate time we must allow them to leave our nest. We must give them to God trusting that they learned from our guidance. We are still parents, we still love our children and we pray that Godly mentors will guide them, but as our roles change the transition is difficult and we agonize over the obvious questions – when is the appropriate time to hand them over to God and how do we find Godly mentors?

A few years ago my daughter, Elizabeth, and I traveled to Zambia with World Hope International. We saw a number of small businesses that World Hope helped incubate. They were transforming communities. One was a banana farm on the banks of the Zambezi River, the massive waterway that spills over Victoria Falls before delineating Zambia and Zimbabwe. The banana farm employed 20 or 30, providing revenue to the community. We toured the farm. We walked past banana trees, saw how they were planted, saw bananas in various stages of growth, saw how they were harvested, and saw fences designed to keep hippopotamuses from trampling the trees.

The hippo fence was near the river. As our guides showed us the fence, I took a step down the bank toward the river and our guide grabbed my arm to stop me. He explained that crocodiles were in the river near the bank. He said they would come up out of the water and attack a person on the bank, and advised me stay to up high. Danger existed that I could not see, and because I had no experience with the situation, the person with experience protected me.

We toured the farm for a few hours, walking between and under trees. Afterward, we sat under a large oak tree and talked. At one point I asked about snakes. I said that had read that king cobras and black mambas were native to the area and I asked if they ever saw snakes like that. They said that they saw both all the time. I asked, "Where do you see them?" They pointed to the banana farm we had just toured for several hours. They said that they see them all the time. I had no idea the danger surrounding us as we walked through the farm. Had I known, the entire experience would have been drastically different.

I did not see the crocodile danger hidden in the river until warned by a person with experience, and I never saw the snake danger surrounding us in the farm. I simply did not have the experience necessary to see the danger. It was not a lack of intelligence, but a lack of experience.

Like parents and children, our guide saw danger that I missed. Parents often see danger that their children overlook because parents have experiences their children do not yet have. We guard them, train them to see indications of danger and teach them to make choices mitigating risk. At some point, we must let go. We must trust that they heard the message, learned from small mistakes, and will make good choices going forward. So we let go, and agonize as we do, and our agony grows as see them make poor choices. Do we step in to help? Do we let them fall? What is our role as our children grow?

I recently spoke with my good friend Jane.[1] We share a bond as parents struggling to sort through our transitioning roles. Jane's son is old enough for her to hand over to the Lord, for her to let go, for her to relinquish, but she continues to see danger on his path that he does not yet see, and she wants to protect him. He wants freedom along with her financial support. She wants to help him financially; she wants him to have the resources he needs to succeed, but she also wants him

---

[1] "Jane" is not her real name.

to heed her guidance. They love each other, but their relationship exhausts them both.

I asked her how her day was going. She said earlier that morning she was really struggling. She felt broken, on the verge of tears with a mix of anger, hopelessness, fear and exhaustion. A woman she did not know called seeking an urgent meeting, and even though Jane did not feel like it, she put on her professional face and attended the meeting. Jane said that when she walked into the meeting, it was as if the woman knew exactly what she was going through. They talked about their children. The woman described her five sons, her trials raising them, and her continued need of turning them over to the Lord. Jane heard "humbling words of her telling me that my son was God's son more than he was mine. God is the Redeemer, the Rescuer, the Salvation, and the Answer, not me. She prayed over me and for my son. She was Jesus in the flesh that day."

They never discussed the business that was so urgent earlier that morning, and the woman has not called Jane again to pursue the once urgent business. Jane never heard from the woman before or since that single encounter. She said, "I left hopeful and humbled and full. It was what I needed for the day."

God placed the woman in Jane's path that day with words of wisdom. God conveyed peace and comfort to Jane through the woman. It was a divine encounter. Jane still struggles with her transitioning role as parent. She continues to pray for guidance regarding the proper balance between her need to release her son to God, her responsibility to help him avoid danger in his path, and the agonizing questions regarding the appropriate time and Godly mentors.

May God's grace fill you. May He give you His peace, comfort, strength, wisdom and discerning Spirit. May you continue to experience the joy of parenthood. And may God send Godly mentors to help our children along the way.

THOUGHTS TO CONSIDER

1. Read Deuteronomy 6:4-9. How do you incorporate your faith into your daily life? What reminders do you have in the places you frequent to focus on God? How do you inspire your children to understand the importance of faith?

2. Read Philippians 4. "Rejoice in the Lord always. I will say it again: Rejoice! Let your gentleness be evident to all. The Lord is near. Do not be anxious about anything, but in everything, by prayer and petition, with thanksgiving, present your requests to God. And the peace of God, which transcends all understanding, will guard your hearts and your minds in Christ Jesus" (Philippians 4:4-7). As you release your child, allowing your child to stand unassisted on his or her feet, where do you place your trust?

3. Read 2 Timothy 3. Paul urges Timothy, his young protégé, "But as for you, continue in what you have learned and have become convinced of, because you know those from whom you learned it, and how from infancy you have known the holy Scriptures, which are able to make you wise for salvation through faith in Christ Jesus" (2 Timothy 3:14-15). Timothy was raised with the solid foundation of God's holy word and he witnessed and experienced the lives of faith around him. What example are you setting for your children? Are you training them in God's holy word so that, when the time comes for you release them, they will have the foundation they

need? What tangible steps should you take to help them grow in faith? Stop and schedule those steps into your day each day over the upcoming week.

4. Read Proverbs 22. "Train a child in the way he should go, and when he is old he will not turn from it" (Proverbs 22:6). Do you see evidence of this principle in your life?

Pantheon, Rome, Italy

14

GOD INCARNATE

In the beginning was the Word, and the Word was with God, and the Word was God. He was with God in the beginning. Through him all things were made; without him nothing was made that has been made. In him was life, and that life was the light of men. The light shines in the darkness, but the darkness has not understood it.... The Word became flesh and made his dwelling among us. We have seen his glory, the glory of the One and Only, who came from the Father, full of grace and truth. John 1:1-5, 1:14

Each Christmas we celebrate one of the most amazing events in human history. "The Word was God... The Word became flesh and made his dwelling among us." God came to earth as a fully human being. Jesus was fully human and fully God. Wrap your mind around that.

When you think of God, what comes to mind? No matter what comes to mind, the thought is too small, too limited, and not grand enough because our mind, our knowledge, our experience, our existence are too human to comprehend God. Even our wildest imagination does not come close. God is that which humans simply cannot fathom.

We say He is holy, divine and pure, but we are unable to comprehend the majesty intended to be communicated by the words because our language is limited and our lens is clouded by sin. We say He has all power, all authority and is the Creator of all things who spoke the universe into existence, who breathes life into each of us, and who delivers order out of chaos, but each concept is too grand for me to wrap my mind around. He is everywhere all at once. He is unbound by space and time. His vision, thinking, reasoning, judgment and discernment are perfect. He is transcendent yet intimate. He knows everything. He knows you and me better than we know ourselves. He is love. He loves us unconditionally.

The words may roll off our tongues easily, but stop for a moment and consider what each designation means because, while I know I am not the smartest person in any room, each one is beyond my ability to comprehend. When Moses met God through the bush that burned yet was not consumed, Moses asked God to tell him His name. Please keep in mind that in that place and time, a person's name meant much more than simply a means of identification, it explained a person's purpose and character, and in some respects knowledge of a person's name provided a degree of power and influence over that person. So Moses' question carried greater significance than it might carry in our society today. God answered, "I am who I am. This is what you are to say to the Israelites: I am has sent me to you" (Exodus 3:14).

That is the only place in Scripture where God's first person name is recorded. It is as if God, by providing an intentionally cryptic response, was explaining that mere mortals are incapable of knowing the Holy, the Divine, the Immortal One. God's name is "I am who I am." Its like the time Samson's father, Manoah, asked an angel his name, and the angel replied, "Why do you ask my name? It is beyond understanding" (Judges 13:18). We humans think we are so advanced, so intelligent, so smart, yet so much is beyond our ability to comprehend.

So God is God. When He desired to create the universe He did so by speaking. He is transcendent and intimate – both beyond our comprehension, right? Now consider this: sovereign, all-powerful God came to earth as, not just a human, but a baby human, the most helpless of beings. The Divine, the Pure, the Holy left heaven and came to this place where evil roams and sin permeates souls. Pause to let that sink in. God became fully human and lived on earth.

After pondering how awesome that is, I am forced to wonder, why would He possibly do that? Scripture quotes Jesus saying over a dozen statements explaining why He came to earth. Let's consider three of them.

> "For I have come down from heaven not to do my will but to do the will of him who sent me. And this is the will of him who sent me, that I shall lose none of all that he has given me, but raise them up on the last day. For my Father's will is that everyone who looks to the Son and believes in him shall have eternal life, and I will raise him up at the last day." John 6:38-40

> "The thief comes only to steal and kill and destroy; I have come that they may have life, and have it to the full." John 10:10

> "I have come into the world as a light, so that no one who believes in me should stay in darkness." John 12:46

Jesus was fully God and fully human. He left heaven, came to earth as a human, and He did so do the Father's will, to provide eternal life, to provide full, abundant life, and to serve as light in the darkness. He came to give each of us the most amazing Christmas gift possible, the gift of His light and life and love.

Take some time to marvel at the magnitude of what Jesus' birth represents. It represents God coming to us, God assuming bodily existence, God seeking a relationship with us, God offering His love, God revealing the way to us. He desires to give each of us, yes you and me, the gift of abundant life, His light, His eternal life. Accept His gift, marvel at His loving grace, praise His holy name, and express awe for His majesty. When you say, hear or see "Merry Christmas!" think of the glory it represents.

Gloria in Excelsis Deo Chapel, Bethlehem, West Bank

THOUGHTS TO CONSIDER

1. Read Genesis 1. "In the beginning God created the heavens and the earth. Now the earth was formless and empty, darkness was over the surface of the deep, and the Spirit of God was hovering over the waters. And God said, 'Let there be light,' and there was light" (Genesis 1:1-3). God created everything out of nothing and He established order out of chaos, all by speaking. Try to imagine the power that action required.

2. Read John 17:1-5. On the evening of the Last Supper, Jesus prayed the chapter-long prayer recorded as chapter 17 of John's Gospel. He begins by praying for Himself and He concludes that portion of the prayer by saying, "And now, Father, glorify me in your presence with the glory I had with you before the world began" (John 17:5). Jesus claims to have shared glory with God the Father before He created the world. This is a claim of deity. He is either God or He was a lunatic. Do you believe, do you know in your heart of hearts that He is God? He sacrificed heavenly glory to come to earth as a human so that we might each be redeemed. What does that mean to you?

3. Paul makes a similar point saying, "For you know the grace of our Lord Jesus Christ, that though he was rich, yet for your sake he became poor, so that you through his poverty might become rich" (2 Corinthians 8:9). Paul uses an economic analogy to convey the magnitude of Jesus' sacrifice for us, though monetary riches pales in comparison to

basking in God's heavenly glory. Imagine other analogies that may convey the amazing reality of God coming to earth as a human. If you were describing this to a present-day congregation, how what analogy would you use?

4. Consider Jesus' mission statement as set forth in the passages from John 6, 10 and 12 above. Describe specific ways Jesus is accomplishing His mission in your life.

Bethlehem, West Bank

15

EYES TO SEE

NOW THERE WAS A MAN IN JERUSALEM CALLED SIMEON, WHO WAS RIGHTEOUS AND DEVOUT. HE WAS WAITING FOR THE CONSOLATION OF ISRAEL, AND THE HOLY SPIRIT WAS ON HIM. IT HAD BEEN REVEALED TO HIM BY THE HOLY SPIRIT THAT HE WOULD NOT DIE BEFORE HE HAD SEEN THE LORD'S CHRIST. MOVED BY THE SPIRIT, HE WENT INTO THE TEMPLE COURTS. WHEN THE PARENTS BROUGHT IN THE CHILD JESUS TO DO FOR HIM WHAT THE CUSTOM OF THE LAW REQUIRED, SIMEON TOOK HIM IN HIS ARMS AND PRAISED GOD, SAYING: "SOVEREIGN LORD, AS YOU HAVE PROMISED, YOU MAY NOW DISMISS YOUR SERVANT IN PEACE. FOR MY EYES HAVE SEEN YOUR SALVATION, WHICH YOU HAVE PREPARED IN THE SIGHT OF ALL PEOPLE, A LIGHT FOR REVELATION TO THE GENTILES, AND THE GLORY OF YOUR PEOPLE ISRAEL."
LUKE 2:25-32

Heavenly forces are at work when we see Jesus for who He is. Beginning with an angel foretelling Jesus' birth to Mary and continuing with the supernatural birth announcement to shepherds, heavenly power and angelic activity surrounded the birth of God in flesh. As Scripture reveals through Simeon, heavenly forces are also at work when we recognize Jesus as God Incarnate.

The Holy Spirit gave Simeon eyes to see Jesus as God's salvation. Others saw baby Jesus, but the Holy Spirit was on

Simeon and when he held the baby, he saw "the consolation of Israel," "the salvation," "the Lord's Messiah," the Son of God. The Holy Spirit opened his eyes to see what others missed, and he immediately recognized Jesus for who He is.

When Peter explained his confidence that Jesus is the Messiah, Jesus said, "Blessed are you, Simon son of Jonah, for this was not revealed to you by man, but by my Father in heaven" (Matthew 16:17). God opened Peter's eyes to see. In the same way, heavenly forces are at work seeking to open our eyes, seeking to allow each of us to see Jesus as God Incarnate, and heaven will accomplish His mission if we only receive God's holy grace.

At the risk of repeating myself too many times over the past few weeks, I will restate the awesome reality of Christmas. God, who gave His first person name to Moses as "I am who I am" (Exodus 3:14), who is beyond our comprehension, who is the almighty, supreme, holy Creator of all things, came to earth as a fully human baby. The holy, divine, pure One came in flesh to this place where evil roams. God, who is unbound by time and space, submitted Himself to human limitations.

What kind of god would do that? We need God, we desire God, our lives are better when lived in communion with God, yet He is beyond our ability to comprehend. Jesus came to earth for many reasons including to help us understand. With a nod to God's first person name, Jesus describes Himself to us in a series of "I am" statements:

> Then Jesus declared, "I am the bread of life. He who *comes to me* will never go hungry, and he who *believes in me* will never be thirsty." John 6:35

> When Jesus spoke again to the people, he said, "I am the light of the world. Whoever *follows me* will never walk in darkness, but will have the light of life." John 8:12

Therefore Jesus said again, "I tell you the truth, I am the gate for the sheep." John 10:7

"I am the good shepherd. The good shepherd *lays down his life* for the sheep." John 10:11

Jesus said to her, "I am the resurrection and the life. He who *believes in me* will live, even though he dies; and whoever lives and believes in me will never die. Do you believe this?" John 11:25-26

Jesus answered, "I am the way and the truth and the life. No one *comes to* the Father except through me." John 14:6

"I am the true vine, and my Father is the gardener. He cuts off every branch in me that bears no fruit, while every branch that does *bear fruit* he prunes, so that it will be even more fruitful…. I am the vine; you are the branches. If a man *remains in me* and I in him, he will *bear much fruit*…." John 15:1-2 & 5

God is the Creator of all things who breathes the breath of life into each of us, and He came to earth bearing gifts for His creation. He is bread for those who are hungry, drink for those who thirst, light for those dwelling in darkness. While describing who He is, He invites us to make use of everything He is offering. He invites us to "come to" Him, "believe in" Him, "follow" Him, "remain in" Him and "bear fruit." In response, He promises to lay down His life, to provide spiritual sustenance and light, and to serve as our path to God.

Jesus simply offers an invitation. While He makes the invitation in several ways on different occasions, He does not insist, He does not attempt to force Himself upon us, He does not twist our arm, He does not beg. He simply offers Himself to us.

May God enlighten the eyes of your spirit to see Jesus in a new and refreshed way. May you gain intimate knowledge of Him in your spirit and soul, may you see Him as God Incarnate, may you allow His glory to transform you, may you respond to His invitation to come, believe, follow, and remain in Him, and may you continue allowing His light to guide your path.

THOUGHTS TO CONSIDER

1. Read Ephesians 1. Paul writes, "I pray also that the eyes of your heart may be enlightened in order that you may know the hope to which he has called you, the riches of his glorious inheritance in the saints, and his incomparably great power for us who believe" (Ephesians 1:18-19). Have you experienced God answering Paul's prayer in your life? If so, how? If not, why do you think that is?

2. Consider each of Jesus' "I am" statements set forth above and the paragraphs in John's Gospel around each statement. For each one, describe in your own words what Jesus means by the statement. How does each one your understanding of Jesus Christ and your faith in Him?

16

Awesome Yet Routine

"If you love me, you will obey what I command. And I will ask the Father, and he will give you another Counselor to be with you forever — the Spirit of truth. The world cannot accept him, because it neither sees him nor knows him. But you know him, for he lives with you and will be in you. I will not leave you as orphans; I will come to you. Before long, the world will not see me anymore, but you will see me. Because I live, you also will live. On that day you will realize that I am in my Father, and you are in me, and I am in you. Whoever has my commands and obeys them, he is the one who loves me. He who loves me will be loved by my Father, and I too will love him and show myself to him.... All this I have spoken while still with you. But the Counselor, the Holy Spirit, whom the Father will send in my name, will teach you all things and will remind you of everything I said to you. Peace I leave with you; my peace I give you. I do not give to you as the world gives. Do not let your hearts be troubled and do not be afraid." John 14:15-21 and 25-27

Garden of Gethsemane, Mount of Olives, Jerusalem, Israel

Twice in the passage above, Jesus connects loving Him to keeping His commands. He provides a clear, concise, objective test: if we truly love Jesus, we will keep His commands. He surrounds the two statements with several promises. He promises the Holy Spirit will be with us forever. He promises, "the world cannot accept [the Holy Spirit]." He also promises the Holy Spirit "will teach you all things and will remind you of everything I said to you." And then Jesus gives His peace. The short passage is loaded with richness and overflowing with awesome promises.

However, some are unable to see. Jesus promises that lots of people in the world will simply be unable to accept the Holy Spirit because He is invisible. In a realm in which most people focus on tangible, material things, spiritual realities may seem untrue, unreal, or insignificant and unworthy of belief. So if you share your faith with folks who are unable to see the truth of your testimony, do not be surprised or deterred because Jesus promises the world is unable to accept the Holy Spirit, the Spirit of truth.

As I watch the sun rise on this beautiful morning, I think about all the ways God reveals His glory to us and through us, and He commonly does so through routine events. We like to share stories describing rare, awesome, miraculous events because they are as if God is reaching out, slapping us in the face and forcing us to see His holy hand at work in real tangible ways. While these are wonderful occurrences that inspire, affirm and strengthen faith, if we focus exclusively on the rare, slap-in-the-face moments, we might overlook the revelation of God's glory through ordinary events.

When you consider the moment of your day worthy of posting on Instagram, do you select the routine, mundane, ordinary moment? Do you post a selfie of yourself sitting in traffic, sitting in your cubicle working on that report that is due later today, folding laundry or putting away dishes? It is the same way with the stories. We discuss stories about God's miraculous touch in a person's life because they describe rare occurrences that, if we choose to believe them, resonate and strengthen our faith. When we believe that God reveals His glory in miraculous ways, our faith grows. Our mountaintop experiences, the times we feel God so close that we can touch, feel and smell Him, are like the best possible vacation photo worthy of posting. It is real and it really happened, and its extraordinariness prepares us to face the ordinary with strengthened faith, renewed peace, refreshed love and opened eyes.

Real life is not revealed in Instagram posts. Real life is our journey through the mundane. For many, life is lived when the alarm goes off earlier than we want, we get ready for our day, we leave for our daily grind, and we return home tired and simply ready to eat and go to bed so we can get up and start it all over again. It is during the routine that we live our faith through prayer, through studying Scripture, by serving others with love, and by allowing God's glory to be revealed through us. We know He is with us. He is here. His holy hand is at work in us, through us and all around us, even during seemingly routine, ordinary, mundane events.

When I experience Him I praise and worship Him because that is the natural response. When I feel distant from Him, I praise and worship Him because I know I need Him, I know I need to focus on prayer, study and service, and I trust that He is with me every step along the way. So long as He is my focus, I will eventually regain experience with Him.

And I trust in His promises. God the Father sends the Holy Spirit to us in Jesus' holy name. He teaches and reminds, and Jesus gives us peace. How awesome is that? As you walk through your daily life, look for the awesome in seemingly ordinary events. God's holy hand is at work and we will see it if we only have eyes to see.

THOUGHTS TO CONSIDER

1. Describe the events surrounding your decision to believe that Jesus Christ is the Savior, the Son of God, who Scripture presents Him to be.

2. When did you accept the Holy Spirit? Why did you do so?

3. Describe other times when you experienced God's holy presence in a real and tangible way.

4. How do your experiences with God influence your faith?

Teaching Steps, Southern Wall, Jerusalem, Israel

17

CALLED TO COMPASSION

IT WAS JUST BEFORE THE PASSOVER FESTIVAL. JESUS KNEW THAT THE HOUR HAD COME FOR HIM TO LEAVE THIS WORLD AND GO TO THE FATHER. HAVING LOVED HIS OWN WHO WERE IN THE WORLD, HE LOVED THEM TO THE END. THE EVENING MEAL WAS BEING SERVED, AND THE DEVIL HAD ALREADY PROMPTED JUDAS ISCARIOT, THE SON OF SIMON, TO BETRAY JESUS. JESUS KNEW THAT THE FATHER HAD PUT ALL THINGS UNDER HIS POWER, AND THAT HE HAD COME FROM GOD AND WAS RETURNING TO GOD; SO HE GOT UP FROM THE MEAL, TOOK OFF HIS OUTER CLOTHING, AND WRAPPED A TOWEL AROUND HIS WAIST. AFTER THAT, HE POURED WATER INTO A BASIN AND BEGAN TO WASH HIS DISCIPLES' FEET, DRYING THEM WITH THE TOWEL THAT WAS WRAPPED AROUND HIM. JOHN 13:1-5

Jesus condenses the Gospel to one word – love. On the evening of the Last Supper, Jesus demonstrated loving service. He donned the wardrobe of a slave and washed the disciples' feet, a job commonly reserved for a slave. He then commanded His disciples to do the same saying,

> "Now that I, your Lord and Teacher, have washed your feet, *you also should wash one another's feet*. I have set you an example that you should do as I have done for you. I tell you the truth, *no servant is greater than his master*, nor is a

messenger greater than the one who sent him. Now that you know these things, *you will be blessed if you do them.*" John 13:14-17

We see Jesus use the phrase "I tell you the truth," Jesus code indicating something very important is about to come. He had just demonstrated a parable in action, and He was about to reveal its significance.

"No servant is greater than his master." If Jesus is our master, and we are His servants, and Jesus assumed the position of a slave, we should assume a position lower than a slave. Jesus is not instructing us to literally wash each other's feet. He is, however, explaining that we should assume the lowest possible position and serve one another by allowing God's love to flow through us as we show compassion to people we encounter.

And we will be blessed if we do these things. We often wonder how to receive God's blessing. Here Jesus tells us how: we do "these things."

Later that evening, Jesus reinforced His call to loving service by saying,

> "A new command I give you: Love one another. *As I have loved you,* so you must love one another. By this all men will know that you are my disciples, if you love one another." John 13:34

He demonstrated loving service by washing feet and He commands love. Now, the command to love one another is not new, and it was not new when Jesus spoke the words. It is as old as Leviticus[iv] and Jesus explained early in His ministry that the command to "love your neighbor as yourself" is the second most important commandment.[v]

So why did Jesus describe it as a "new"? He said, "As I have loved you." He had just demonstrated loving service through a parable in action by assuming the position of a slave and serving with compassion, and He was about to demonstrate His love by laying down His life for us. By saying, "As I have loved you," Jesus changed the command in a radical way, and if you think it through to its core, the only possible way any human may come close to loving the way Jesus loves is by allowing Jesus' love to flow through them.

But where do we begin? How do we begin? It starts with God and ends with God. As we bow to worship Him, we see Christ Jesus for who He is, we submit to His authority and recognize that everyone around us is created in God's image, is loved by God, and is worthy of our loving compassion. We realize that serving other people is a form of worshiping God, and we begin to realize that our social position is not nearly as important as serving others. In fact, any position of influence we may have is only significant to the extent we use that position to help others, to show compassion to others and to allow Jesus' love to flow through us.

May God enlighten the eyes of your spirit to see opportunities around you to offer your loving compassion to others, and when you see the opportunity, may He give you His courage, power and strength to carry step out in love.

Thoughts to Consider

1.   Considering that Jesus washing the disciples' feet was a parable in action, what might He have done today in our culture to make the same point?

2.   What actions have you taken over the past week to offer compassionate, loving service to another? How did you feel after serving?

3.   Did you notice any opportunities arise where you might have served, but chose not to? Describe the situation. What caused you to say, "No"? How did you feel after saying, "No"?

4.   Read John 10:7-10. Jesus describes Himself as the gate, then He compares Himself to the thief. The thief comes to "steal and kill and destroy" while Jesus came "that they may have life, and have it to the full" (John 10:10). How is the act of compassionate, loving service connected to the full life offered through Jesus Christ?

Saint Peter's Basilica, Vatican City

Randy L. Allen

18

HOLY LIVING SACRIFICE

THEREFORE, I URGE YOU, BROTHERS, IN VIEW OF GOD'S MERCY, TO OFFER YOUR BODIES AS LIVING SACRIFICES, HOLY AND PLEASING TO GOD – THIS IS YOUR SPIRITUAL ACT OF WORSHIP. DO NOT CONFORM ANY LONGER TO THE PATTERN OF THIS WORLD, BUT BE TRANSFORMED BY THE RENEWING OF YOUR MIND. THEN YOU WILL BE ABLE TO TEST AND APPROVE WHAT GOD'S WILL IS – HIS GOOD, PLEASING AND PERFECT WILL. ROMANS 12:1-2

Saint Paul's Basilica Outside the Walls, Rome, Italy

The passage is tightly packed and rich with meaning. Three short sentences discuss God's mercy, true and proper worship, the pattern of the world, transformation of our minds, and God's will.

As we see here, Scripture often discusses the world in contrast to the heavenly. In other places God's holy word discusses the world as "this dark world"[vi] and the "the dominion of darkness."[vii] Peter describes the world as the place where Satan prowls like a lion seeking people to devour.[viii] Jesus says He saw Satan fall from heaven like lightning.[ix] Where did he fall? The Book of Job causes us to conclude that he fell to earth where he roams.[x] Paul refers to the worldly in contrast to the heavenly, and urges us not to conform to the patterns of the world, but to seek heavenly influences and to be transformed by them.

We live in a realm exhibiting great contrast. We see evidence of both evil and holiness. God's holy word urges us to seek God and His holiness, to "offer your bodies as living sacrifices, holy and pleasing to God" and to "be transformed by the renewing of your mind." As we move towards God He transforms us, we gain bits of holiness, we gain eyes to see other people as beings created in God's holy image and we take on God's desire to offer compassionate loving service to them.

At first glance it seems inconsistent, but we must act while we surrender. Surrender often entails ceasing activity, but not here. Our limited part of the equation boils down to study, prayer and service. As we seek Him through prayer and by studying His holy word, our minds are renewed, our relationship with Him is strengthened, and we desire to serve others. We seek Him, we surrender to Him, and we allow Him to guide our actions as we serve Him. As we perform our limited part, we allow God to have His way with us.

And Scripture promises that as a result our transformation, we will understand God's will. Pause and consider this awesome truth for a moment.

For many, this happens gradually as we inch along the path towards holiness, as we seek Him, as we identify influences in our lives that hinder our growth towards Him and eliminate those influences from our lives, and as we continue to inch closer to Him (or as we continue to allow more of Him in, whichever image works better for you). Rather than conforming to the patterns of this dark world, we should "be transformed by the renewing of [our minds]."

Spiritual transformation creates the desire to serve and service is worship – we are offering ourselves as a living sacrifice to God for His use. He urges us to offer our "bodies as living sacrifices, holy and pleasing to God" as our "spiritual act of worship." Holy, living sacrifice. Only God is holy, and while we may never be holy, we step towards holiness through the spiritual transformation available to us through Him. And as we progress towards holiness, our transformation reveals itself through our actions. Here, God's holy word captures the message of the Gospel in three words – holy living sacrifice. Spiritual transformation displayed through action.

I recently spoke with a friend who works as a counselor to clients in recovery. He discussed the need for action. He said for a person in recovery, it is one thing to have the intellectual knowledge about the disease of addiction, and the intellectual knowledge of what to do every day to avoid relapse, but the knowledge is incomplete if it is not put into practice. And so it is with faith. If our faith is purely intellectual, it is incomplete and so long as it is purely intellectual it is arguably not really faith. We must put our faith in action.

Holy, living sacrifice is a standard remarkable for many reasons, including its inherent contrast. Holiness implies being sanctified or set apart. Living sacrifice implies serving others, which requires close interaction. It calls for us to be set apart from the world as holy, yet thrust into the world as servants revealing God's love. We are called to be salt adding holy flavor to the world.[xi] We are also called to be holy light illuminating the path of the dark world, set apart yet mixed in offering loving service.[xii]

Perhaps because it is such a remarkable standard, each time we take Holy Communion, we pray offering ourselves as holy, living sacrifices to God. I love the opportunity to take Holy Communion, to dine with others at the Lord's Table. I love it because when I swallow the elements and feel them go down my throat, I feel God's Holy Presence enter me, strengthen me and refresh me. I feel His holy presence in a new way. The mystery of His spiritual presence takes tangible form and that seemingly insignificant act is the source of incredible inspiration that is enhanced when shared with others.

The United Methodist Hymnal provides a basic order of worship for different types of church services, including Holy Communion. When we take Holy Communion we recreate some of the events that took place during the Last Supper. As we pray, we take bread, break it, and we recite the words that Jesus spoke saying, "Take, eat, this is my body which is given for you. Do this in remembrance of me."[xiii] We take a cup of grape juice and recite the words that Jesus spoke saying, "Drink from this all of you; this is my blood of the new covenant, poured out for you and for many for the forgiveness of sins. Do this, as often as you drink it, in remembrance of me."[xiv]

We continue praying saying, "And so, in remembrance of these your mighty acts in Jesus Christ, we offer ourselves in praise and thanksgiving as a holy and living sacrifice, in union with Christ's offering for us, as we proclaim the mystery of faith."[xv]

Each time we take Holy Communion using the regular order of worship, we renew our offer to God. We ask Him to accept us as a holy and living sacrifice. We offer ourselves as holy. We offer ourselves as living sacrifices.

A great deal of Scripture is about spiritual life, God's desire for us to allow Him to transform us, the avenues through which we may connect with God, and the revelation of God's glory. As wonderful as it might be to experience God's glory, to bask in His light, to commune with Him, and to experience the change, He does not offer His gift of grace purely for our pleasure. He offers His gift of grace to transform us and through that transformation, to position us for His service. He reveals His glory to the world in many ways including through His creation, through His word and through His people. If we desire satisfaction, if we desire a full, enriched, meaningful life, if we desire life abundant, we must allow God to transform our spirits and souls, we must allow God's love to fill us and flow through us, and we must act in the world revealing His love and His glory. We each must offer ourselves as a holy, living sacrifice.

May God's light shine upon you, may you have eyes to see and ears to hear, may your heart be fertile soil for His holy seed to grow, may His glory continue to be revealed through you.

Thoughts to Consider

1. Read Exodus 19:1-6. Three months after leading the Israelites out of Egypt, God urges them to recognize His holy hand at work and to trust that He will continue acting on their behalf and He asks them to engage in relationship with Him. Do you see parallels to the passage above from Romans?

2. Read 1 Peter 2:1-5. List specific ways this passage meshes with the passages from Exodus and Romans above.

3.   Read John 13. Jesus says it is all about love. While Paul condenses the Gospel down to three words – holy, living sacrifice – Jesus condenses it to one – love. Describe how the messages support one another.

Damascus Gate, Jerusalem, Israel

19

STUMBLING BLOCKS

SOME OF THE ELDERS OF ISRAEL CAME TO ME AND SAT DOWN IN FRONT OF ME. THEN THE WORD OF THE LORD CAME TO ME: "SON OF MAN, THESE MEN HAVE SET UP IDOLS IN THEIR HEARTS AND PUT WICKED STUMBLING BLOCKS BEFORE THEIR FACES. SHOULD I LET THEM INQUIRE OF ME AT ALL? THEREFORE SPEAK TO THEM AND TELL THEM, 'THIS IS WHAT THE SOVEREIGN LORD SAYS: WHEN ANY ISRAELITE SETS UP IDOLS IN HIS HEART AND PUTS A WICKED STUMBLING BLOCK BEFORE HIS FACE AND THEN GO TO A PROPHET, I THE LORD WILL ANSWER HIM MYSELF IN KEEPING WITH HIS GREAT IDOLATRY. I WILL DO THIS TO RECAPTURE THE HEARTS OF THE PEOPLE OF ISRAEL, WHO HAVE ALL DESERTED ME FOR THEIR IDOLS.'"
EZEKIEL 14:1-5

Scripture uses the term "stumbling blocks" as things in our lives that hinder our progression towards God or prevent us from serving Him according to His call. They cause us to stumble. In places Scripture describes people acting as stumbling blocks to others. In other passages, situations surrounding a person become a stumbling block, and in others, people choose to place stumbling blocks in their own path.

The passage above presents the latter type. Through the prophet Ezekiel, God warns that He will judge each person who "sets up idols in his heart and puts a wicked stumbling block before his face," and He explains that His response will be designed to bring each person back to Him. If we are heading in the wrong direction and we turn back to God and begin progressing towards Him, that is repentance. So God's response will be designed to elicit repentance.

The men in the story seem upstanding. They are elders of Israel who seek the prophet's counsel. They meet with Ezekiel and sit before him as he addresses them. Outwardly they seem respectful, reverent and appropriate. But God knows each of our hearts. God knows us better than we know ourselves and He told Ezekiel what was in their hearts. They looked and acted the part, but they secretly held idols in the dark recesses of their hearts and they placed stumbling blocks in front of themselves.

Earlier, God explained through Ezekiel that gold and silver caused Israel to stumble (see Ezekiel 7:19). Pride, ambition, self-confidence, wealth and the pursuit of personal pleasure had become their idols, and the gold and silver that surrounded them became their stumbling block. They pursued the trappings of wealth rather than God.

On one occasion Jesus accuses Peter of acting like a stumbling block to Jesus, indicating that one person might be a stumbling to another. Jesus and the disciples are in Caesarea Philippi. Peter confesses that he knows Jesus is the Messiah and Jesus explains that Peter's knowledge is a gift from God. After that, Jesus explains that He must go to Jerusalem where He will be killed and on the third day raised. Hearing those words, Peter says, "Never, Lord! This shall never happen to you." Jesus turns to Peter and says, "Get behind me, Satan! You are a stumbling block to me; you do not have in mind the things of God, but the things of men" (see Matthew 16:13-23).

Jesus had just commended Peter for hearing and listening to God the Father. Peter had information only available from God and Jesus applauded Peter for this significant step. In His next breath, Jesus refers to Peter as "Satan" and a "stumbling block" because Peter's mind is focused on human things rather than divine things. Jesus urges Peter and us to focus on divine things.

Jesus makes it sound so easy, but we know it is not. We possess great contrast within us. We have the Holy Spirit dwelling within us, transforming us into holiness. We also have human inclinations and are influenced by evil. Peter's desire to save his close friend from suffering was not an evil desire, it was merely human and not divine. Jesus urges us to focus on the divine, which is only possible through the indwelling Holy Spirit and His transformation.

Jesus provides the recipe for correcting this problem. Scripture continues:

> Then Jesus said to his disciples: "If anyone would come after me, he must deny himself and take up his cross and follow me. For whoever wants to save his life will lose it, but whoever loses his life for me will find it. What good will it be for a man if he gains the whole world, yet forfeits his soul? Or what can a man give in exchange for his soul? Matthew 16:24-26

The recipe involves self-denial. It is about surrendering our ambition, our selfish desires, our pride, and replacing all that with the desire to know God, to engage in relationship with God, and to serve God.

Jesus described Peter as a stumbling block because he was trying to convince Jesus to avoid the task that God called Him to. Peter's intentions were good by human standards, but they were inconsistent with God's plan.

The elders who met with Ezekiel had allowed their pursuit of wealth, their pride, their ambition, and their pursuit of personal pleasure to block them from God. They desired all that rather than God. All that was their idol and their desires were their stumbling block.

What is your stumbling block? What separates you from God? What prevents you from following through on the task He has set before you to accomplish?

May God reveal the obstacles to you, may He grant you His courage, strength and endurance to remove them from your path, and may He continue to reveal His glory through you.

Thoughts to Consider

1.   Read Isaiah 1. What are the people doing that has angered God in the passage? What parallel exists between Isaiah 1 and Ezekiel 14? What might we be guilty of doing today that might be evoking God's anger?

2.   Read Jeremiah 11 with particular attention to verse 11. Why has God stopped listening to their cries? Do you see any similarities to your life?

3.   Read Romans 14:13. Is it possible you have been a stumbling block to people around you? How so? In light of this realization, what should you change?

4.   Read Colossians 3:1-15. God's holy word urges us to set our minds on "things above, not on earthly things" (Colossians 3:2). What specific guidance does the passage present to help us do so? How might you apply the instruction to your life?

Corinth Canal, Isthmus of Corinth, Greece

20

STRONGHOLDS

INDEED, WE LIVE AS HUMAN BEINGS, BUT WE DO
NOT WAGE WAR ACCORDING TO HUMAN
STANDARDS; FOR THE WEAPONS OF OUR WARFARE
ARE NOT MERELY HUMAN, BUT THEY HAVE DIVINE
POWER TO DESTROY STRONGHOLDS. WE DESTROY
ARGUMENTS AND EVERY PROUD OBSTACLE RAISED UP
AGAINST THE KNOWLEDGE OF GOD, AND WE TAKE
EVERY THOUGHT CAPTIVE TO OBEY CHRIST. 2
CORINTHIANS 10:3-5 (NRSV)

"The weapons of *our* warfare are not merely human, but they have *divine power* to destroy strongholds." Whose warfare is it? It is ours. We have human weapons at our disposal as well as weapons with divine power to destroy strongholds. That is worth repeating. We have divine power at our disposal to destroy strongholds.

What does Paul mean by strongholds? Writing in Greek, Paul used the word transliterated as ochuroma, which means a secure, heavily fortified military fortress. It is a walled, armed safe place to protect people from attack.

An example from Paul's time was the fortress built by Herod known as the Masada. From about 37 BC until 31 BC, Herod built a fortress on a tall plateau by the Dead Sea about 60 miles south of Jerusalem. On the short side the cliffs are 300 feet high. On the tall side the cliffs are 1300 feet high. Herod stocked the fortress with supplies to last a long time. He designed the

Masada to be his refuge in the event he was ever attacked. About 100 years after Herod designed the fortress, a group of Jewish zealots sought refuge there. The fortress was inaccessible, so when the Roman army arrived seeking the people who occupied it, they began by surrounding the plateau. The fortress, the place of refuge, suddenly became a jail.

In the context of Paul's original writing, Paul uses the word ochuroma, stronghold or fortress figuratively. The word refers to false "arguments and proud obstacles raised up against the knowledge of God" – arguments raised by his critics as fortresses in which they are seeking to avoid reality, seeking to avoid the truth, seeking to remain in denial of the Gospel. Paul is confronting purveyors of false doctrine.

God's holy word is the living word. He speaks to us through His word. God makes promises to us through His word, and He promises that He speaks His word with a purpose and "it shall not return to [Him] empty" (Isaiah 55:11, NRSV).

As I read God's holy word today – words about strongholds, arguments, proud obstacles raised up against the knowledge of God – I see strongholds as anything in our lives that prevent us from growing closer to God. Strongholds are things in our lives that hold us where we are, and prevent us from moving forward along the path towards God. They are fortresses holding us hostage, and pride is at the foundation of many of them.

In my experience, as we escape one stronghold we find ourselves bound by another, which we must escape. They are different for each of us. The number and variety of conditions holding us hostage are as numerous and varied as the conditions of each human heart – they seem infinite.

What separates you from God? What prevents you from moving along the path towards God? What prevents you from serving God?

Worry? Fear? Doubt? I am reminded of sleepless nights, tossing and turning in agony over the decisions I saw my child make, the destruction of his future opportunities, and my inability to effectuate change. I knew that my sleeplessness helped nothing, nonetheless, I continued tossing and turning night after night. I prayed and prayed and finally I surrendered, seeking balance between my responsibility and proper role as parent, and my need to surrender to God.

Is it grief, pain and suffering? They are elements of our human condition. Grief, pain and suffering are, to some extent, part of our existence here on earth. We each respond in our own way. For some, grief, pain and suffering cause us to grow closer to God while others move in the opposite direction. Asking "why?" is natural. Questions are good. But some, after asking good questions conclude that a loving God would not allow the grief, pain or suffering that they experience, so either God is not loving or God does not exist, and either way they choose to stop worshiping, to stop following, to stop believing. Grief, pain and suffering become, rather than avenues to see God's glory in a new and refreshed way, rather than opportunities to grow closer to God, they becomes a strongholds separating them from God.

I heard a story on the radio recently about two people and their opposite reactions to the same events. A man had leukemia. He sought treatment at MD Anderson in Houston and he entered a database seeking a blood donor. As he waited for a match he underwent conventional treatment and his health rapidly declined, his pain and suffering rapidly increased and as he prayed for help that did not come his faith began to falter. Then one day he received a call. Out of 8 million people in the database they found his perfect match. A single person out of 8 million, and her blood saved him. He saw God's fingerprint all over the situation. He saw God's glory. His faith grew. He experienced God giving him new life.

But the woman who donated her blood is an atheist. She does not see God in any of it.

For the man, his suffering and pain was creating doubt that could have become a stronghold, but through prayer he had eyes to see God's glory, he had eyes to see God's miraculous fingerprint over the situation. For the woman, something continues to separate her from God.

Is it possible your self-confidence is a stronghold? For many their confidence that they have earned their possessions, lifestyle and position on their own becomes a stronghold. This is as old as the Psalms. In Psalm 10 David writes about prosperous people who are unable to see God because they are blinded by their riches.

For many in our culture, the stronghold has its roots in the so-called American Dream and our reverence for the self-made man. It is rooted in the myth of independence. We really believe we are doing it all on our own, and through that myth we convince ourselves that we really have no need for God. We hear the intellectual arguments, we might even accept intellectually that God is the Creator of all things, but when we look at our home, car and bank account we believe that we earned all that by our own hard work and we cannot convince ourselves that God had any role in it. Is it possible that your self-confidence and your worldview are your strongholds?

As we see new headlines published daily, we read about more and more people who have abused the power of their position. They were granted certain power and privilege to perform a job on behalf of their employer, and they used that power and privilege for their personal pleasure, leaving a wake of carnage in their path. Their pursuit of personal pleasure became a stronghold.

For many a stronghold is the pursuit of pleasure or some form of addiction. Porn is a multi-billion dollar business. It does not generate that much revenue without lots of demand, lots of use, and lots of people willing to pay for it. It is a trap for many. Substance abuse and substance-related addiction impacts virtually everyone. Almost every family is impacted by addiction.

We each have things in our lives separating us from God and preventing us from serving God as He calls us to serve Him, but God's holy word promises that He gives us His "divine power to destroy strongholds." As we identify a stronghold and deploy divine power to destroy it, we will likely encounter another one and another one as we walk our path of faith towards God. No matter what you are facing, God is with you and you possess "divine power to destroy strongholds."

May you have eyes to see your stronghold and when you identify it, may you receive God's courage, strength, and power to destroy it.

Stone at Caesarea Maritime, Israel

THOUGHTS TO CONSIDER

1. Read Psalm 4. David feels separated from God and he cries out to God for help. God calls out His people for "turning [His] glory into shame," for loving delusions and seeking false gods (Psalm 4:2). David concludes saying, "I will lie down and sleep in peace, for you alone, Lord, make me dwell in safety" (Psalm 4:8). When have you cried out to God for help? Describe how He communicated His assurance to you that He is with you, that He is the source of your safety?

2. Read Psalm 10. The psalmist describes the ways of wicked people and concludes trusting that God hears our prayers, encourages us and defends us. How does the passage mesh with the passage from 1 Corinthians above?

3. Think back to times in your life when you were held in bondage. How did God deliver you? What role did you play in your deliverance? How did you make use of divine power?

21

DIVINE POWER TO DESTROY STRONGHOLDS

INDEED, WE LIVE AS HUMAN BEINGS, BUT WE DO NOT WAGE WAR ACCORDING TO HUMAN STANDARDS; FOR THE WEAPONS OF OUR WARFARE ARE NOT MERELY HUMAN, BUT THEY HAVE DIVINE POWER TO DESTROY STRONGHOLDS. WE DESTROY ARGUMENTS AND EVERY PROUD OBSTACLE RAISED UP AGAINST THE KNOWLEDGE OF GOD, AND WE TAKE EVERY THOUGHT CAPTIVE TO OBEY CHRIST. 2 CORINTHIANS 10:3-5 (NRSV)

Great Theater, Ephesus, Turkey

Strongholds are things in our lives holding us where we are, blocking our progression towards God and preventing us from serving God as He calls us. Often we find pride at the foundation of strongholds.

God directed my attention to the passage above during a recent prayer meeting. We met in the Sanctuary, discussed prayer concerns and then separated for a time of individual prayer. People scattered around the Sanctuary to pray. I knelt directly in front of the pulpit, and as I prayed "pride" kept coming to me. Over and over the word "pride" kept appearing in my mind. After fifteen minutes or so we started gathering back together. Freddie had been in the balcony praying. As she walked up carrying a Bible she said, "Pastor, God led me to a verse that I want to share with you." She handed me the Bible and pointed to 2 Corinthians 10:5-6 (NRSV), directing my eyes to "proud obstacle." I told her that the word "pride" kept coming to me as I prayed. She said she also prayed about pride. As I read the passage, Morgan walked up. He had been in the back of the Sanctuary praying. Freddie told him what had happened. He said that he had also been praying about pride.

As we met in that sacred, consecrated space, as we worshiped, prayed and sought God together, He directed our attention to pride and to a specific line of Scripture on that topic. What are we to do with this? Is our pride a stronghold?

Surrender is the opposite of pride. Several friends who are active in the recovery community have expressed to me the thought that surrendering pride is essential to lasting recovery. They each revealed stories to demonstrate this point, which in most instances started with an explanation of the time they hit rock bottom, the lowest point that they could imagine achieving. Each story is unique, but they share a common element. After trying unsuccessfully time and time again to gain control over their lives using their own power, they continued to sink lower and lower until finally reaching a point lower than they imagined sinking to, which is when they finally surrender. They submit to God. They relinquish control and after they surrender they begin to move closer to Him. Through brokenness they finally surrender pride, and through surrender they find God's healing power.

While you may not be recovering from addiction, we are each recovering from our sinful nature. Something or possibly many things separate each of us from God, and we each need to surrender our pride as we submit to God. As Jesus begins the Sermon on the Mount He says, "Blessed are the poor in spirit for theirs is the kingdom of heaven" (Matthew 5:3). God offers a special blessing to people who are spiritually broken. To be poor in spirit is to be fully surrendered, emptied of self, emptied of pride. It involves surrendering our ambition and desire, and replacing all that with a longing for God and a desire to serve Him. In one of his letters to Timothy, Paul urges him, and us, to surrender himself fully to God, urging him to be a cleansed vessel, emptied of worldliness, made holy, set aside to be filled by God (see 2 Timothy 2:20-22). And so it is for us.

If strongholds are things separating each of us from God, and we have at our disposal weapons of "divine power to destroy strongholds," what are these weapons, how do we access them, and how do we deploy them?

It is likely that Paul is referring to the same concept that he discussed in a previous letter to the same folks. At 1 Corinthians 2:4-5 Paul writes, "My speech and my proclamation were not with plausible words of wisdom, but with a demonstration of the Spirit and power, so that your faith might rest not on human wisdom but on the power of God (NRSV)." He refers to the power of the Holy Spirit. He refers to God's power.

And at Ephesians 6:10-18, Paul discusses battles taking place in the spiritual realm. He discusses forces of evil battling heavenly forces. He urges us to "put on the full armor of God" (Ephesians 6:11), which he describes as truth and righteousness firmly based on the Gospel of peace, the shield of faith and the helmet of salvation. After discussing tools available to defend us from attack, Paul discusses a single weapon – the sword of the Holy Spirit, which is the word of God. He finishes the thought by urging us to "pray in the Spirit on all occasions with all kinds of prayers and requests" (Ephesians 6:18).

So what is the weapon with divine power? It is God's power made available through the Holy Spirit, God's holy word and prayer. It is the power of the Holy Spirit, "the sword of the Spirit, which is the word of God" accessed through prayer.

We know there is power in the Name of Jesus,[xvi] but do we use it? Do we use the divine power available to us? When you feel the tug of strongholds, when you feel the urge of temptation, call on the divine power available to you. Call on the sword of the Holy Spirit, deploy the power of Jesus' holy name, use the power of the word, pray. The urge of temptation is a reminder to pray, to study Scripture, to serve others.

We live as human beings. We live as humans here on earth bound by time and space, yet God grants us use of weapons with divine power to destroy strongholds. We have access to divine power. We have the sword of the Holy Spirit. We have the word of God. We have access to divine power.

I urge you to seize God's promises. Make use of His divine power. Stake your claim to the sword of the Holy Spirit, the word of God, and the power of prayer. May God's glory continue to be revealed through you.

THOUGHTS TO CONSIDER

1. Jesus says, "I tell you the truth, my Father will give you whatever you ask in my name" (John 16:23). He says, "And I will do whatever you ask in my name, so that the Son may bring glory to the Father" (John

14:13). He also says, "I have given you authority to trample on snakes and scorpions and to overcome all the power of the enemy; nothing will harm you" (Luke 10:19). How do these images of power fit with the passage from 2 Corinthians first set forth above?

2. Read 2 Timothy 2 with particular attention to verses 20-21. What is your daily ritual to cleanse yourself for holiness?

3. Read Ephesians 6. How does the chapter influence your view of the spiritual realm surrounding us and influencing us, and of your spirituality?

4. God's holy word promises that you have divine power to destroy strongholds. What specific steps will you take this week to identify a stronghold and to deploy divine power to destroy it?

22

A Prayer for Unity

I ASK NOT ONLY ON BEHALF OF THESE, BUT ALSO ON BEHALF OF THOSE WHO WILL BELIEVE IN ME THROUGH THEIR WORD, THAT THEY MAY ALL BE ONE. AS YOU, FATHER, ARE IN ME AND I AM IN YOU, MAY THEY ALSO BE IN US, SO THAT THE WORLD MAY BELIEVE THAT YOU HAVE SENT ME. THE GLORY THAT YOU HAVE GIVEN ME I HAVE GIVEN THEM, SO THAT THEY MAY BE ONE, AS WE ARE ONE, I IN THEM AND YOU IN ME, THAT THEY MAY BECOME COMPLETELY ONE, SO THAT THE WORLD MAY KNOW THAT YOU HAVE SENT ME AND HAVE LOVED THEM EVEN AS YOU HAVE LOVED ME. JOHN 17:20-23 (NRSV)

I recently read with new eyes John 17, the chapter long prayer prayed by Jesus. I was struck by it because here we are, living in a time described as the Age of Discord while people around us cry out for unity, and John tells us that 2,000 years ago Jesus prayed for us. He prayed that we might find unity.

On the evening of the Last Supper, the evening that Jesus gave Himself up for us, He taught at a frenzied pace. He taught amazing lesson after amazing lesson recorded at John 13 through 17 – 5 chapters of amazing teaching. He knew what was about to happen. He knew His relationship with the disciples was about to change radically, so He tried to explain so much. Like the night before a final exam – after a full semester there was so much I still needed to cram in at the last minute.

For the disciples, even after years living and working together, there was still so much that Jesus needed to say. At one point in the evening Jesus said, "I have much more to say to you, more than you can now bear" (John 16:12).

Jesus washed the disciples feet, taught them about loving service and told them to do likewise. Jesus explained who the Holy Spirit is and promised that the Holy Spirit teaches all things and brings peace. He taught about the vine and the branches and He gave a new command telling us to love one another as He has loved us. And He taught so much more.

He taught about loving service and love and the Holy Spirit. He told us to abide in God and to allow God to abide in us, and He commanded us to love one another. And after all this, the culmination of His teaching was a prayer. His amazing prayer fills an entire chapter. He starts by praying for Himself. Then He prays for the disciples. After that He prays for us, the people who come to believe through disciples.

This is so amazing to me. Jesus knows what is about to happen, and He teaches at a frenzied pace and, in the middle of all this, He takes the time to pray for us. What does He pray at this most urgent, most important time?

2,000 years ago, a few hours before Jesus was arrested, Jesus prayed for us and His primary concern was our unity. In three sentences set forth above He prays for our unity three times.

1. <u>One with Each Other</u>. He prays that we, the Body of Christ, might be one with each other in the same way that Jesus is one with the Father. Let that sink in for a minute. Try to imagine how close Jesus is to the Father. They are one. They are two parts of the Holy Trinity. God is one God in three persons. They are two of the same one. They are closer than we are able to comprehend, and Jesus prays that we will be that close with one another.

2. <u>One with God</u>. In verse 21 Jesus prays that we will be in God, so that the world will believe that Jesus is the Messiah. Earlier in the evening Jesus taught about the vine and the branches and He urges us to abide in Him and allow Him to abide in us. He describes a perfectly symbiotic relationship where Jesus is the vine, we are the branches and so long as we abide in Him, allowing His sustenance to flow through us, fruit will be produced through us, the branches. Then He says, "abide in my love" and He commands us to "love each other" as He has loved us (see John 15:1-17, NRSV). His prayer is a continuation of His teaching, ideally brought to life.

3. <u>So that the world may believe</u>. He says "so that the world may believe" and "so that the world may know" (v.21&23, NRSV). Jesus prays for unity between people and unity between each person and Him, but unity is not the goal. He prays for unity as a tool with a purpose – through unity we may serve as witness to the world. We make up one body, the Body of Christ. That Body, the church, the movement of believers serves as witness to the world, but only if its members are united together and united with Christ. Jesus prays for us, He prays for our unity so that we are able to be witnesses to Him. We are called with a purpose and that purpose is to bring glory to God. He gives us His glory to help the world believe and as a result, to glorify Him.

4. <u>Glory</u>. In verse 22 Jesus prays, "*The glory* that you have given me I have given them ... (NRSV)." The glory

helps us with the first two prayers – to be one with each other and one with God.

What is the glory? He has given it to us, but what is it? And how does it help us? The glory is the earthly manifestation of God; at times it is His Holy Spirit within our spirit revealing Himself in a real and tangible way through our actions. The instant we find Jesus Christ and accept Him as our Lord and Savior, the Holy Spirit enters us, we are justified, and we started the long journey in the direction of sanctification. Along that journey, we take on more and more of the Holy Spirit and we leave, little by little, our human spirit behind.

But the glory is the manifestation of God's holy presence and the Holy Spirit allows all of this to happen. The Holy Spirit allows us to be one with each other, and the Holy Spirit allows us to be one with God the Father and Jesus.

I know I'm going to go out on a limb here … but I nonetheless say that this is the coolest thing you will hear today – it is so cool that Jesus prays for you. He prays for me. He prays for us. The Holy Spirit prays for us now (see Romans 8:26). And His glory is in you and revealed through you. May you continue to abide in Him and He in you, and may we be united as one Body of Christ.

THOUGHTS TO CONSIDER

1. When have you felt the closest to God the Father and Jesus Christ? Where were you? Who were you with? What were you doing? Have you ever tried to replicate that moment?

2. When do you feel the closest to other people? Describe a particular moment of unity with another

person. Where were you? Who were you with?
What were you doing? Have you ever tried to
replicate that moment?

3. How might unity among followers of Christ cause
others to believe that Jesus is the Christ? Have you
experienced evidence of that happening?

Patmos, Greece

23

A Prayer for Unity – Part II

"Righteous Father, though the world does not know you, I know you, and they know that you have sent me. I have made you known to them, and will continue to make you known in order that the love you have for me may be in them and that I myself may be in them." John 17:25-26

Mount Hermon

The land known as the Holy Land has a history of conflict, violence and strife. Like the world around us, the Holy Land is filled with great contrast – places where Jesus likely stood, places marked by God's glory, places where Biblical accounts occurred, and also signs of war.

We traveled north from the Sea of Galilee. As we inched closer to Mount Hermon, the temperature dropped, the wind grew, and signs of past conflict and current preparations for the possibility of conflict were increasingly evident. My map indicated we were in Syria, but tangible evidence on the ground showed we were still in Israel – the Israeli flag flew over military installations, Israeli tanks and armored vehicles traveled and sat alongside the road, Israeli and UN soldiers patrolled, a tall fence topped with concertina wire stood to the east indicating the physical barrier separating Syria and Israel, a Syrian flag flew over the town east of the fence, and guard towers, barricades and bunkers littered the landscape. It was a peaceful day but edginess was apparent indicating peace could be shattered at any moment.

We stood on the foothills of Mount Hermon, the likely sight of Jesus' transfiguration, admiring the beauty of the snow-covered mountain and imagining with new eyes the majesty of the transfiguration, all while surrounded by tangible evidence of human discord. Our world is a place of great contrast – it is the place where God reveals His glory and also the place where Satan roams and great evil exists – and the world's contrast was evident in this place in a single snapshot.

Our guide, Jimmy, said the valley was known by a name translated as the Valley of the Shouting. When the fence separated families, they went close to the fence and shouted to one another seeking updates on family they could no longer see.

Following the example set by Jesus in John 17, we prayed for unity, we prayed for peace, we prayed for bonds of trust to be re-established, we prayed for the spirit of forgiveness to invade and transform each person.

Lori with Mount Hermon in background

The message Jesus taught on the evening of the Last Supper focused on relationships. He started demonstrating loving service, He commanded love, He discussed abiding in God, and He discussed the possibility of relationship with the Holy Spirit. After all that, He prayed for unity. His message focused on relationships between us and God, and us and each other, and His prayer focused on unity.

Isn't it quite a coincidence that the two greatest commandments are 1) love God with all your heart, soul, mind and strength; and 2) love your neighbor as yourself?

We are called to be relational. We are called to worship God together. We are called to be the Body of Christ. We are called to be His holy church. We cannot do any of this as individuals; we can only do it together. But we must be together. We must be united.

As we seek unity, please know that unity is not natural. Scientific laws describe the natural order – how things happen in nature. The Second Law of Thermodynamics, the Law of Entropy, tells us that systems move irreversibly from order toward disorder, from neat and systematic towards chaotic and random, from unity towards separation. And this Law tells us that energy and molecules and systems move irreversibly toward randomness until an intervening force changes the path and provides order and unity. So the natural state, left to itself, moves increasingly towards chaos.

Unity is not natural; it requires an intervening force. Unity is supernatural. Unity requires God.

Unity is not natural, yet we humans seek it. Think of all the protest signs you may have seen on the news or in newspaper photos calling out for unity. People across the world seek unity. Whether they realize it or not, this is a cry out for God. If we seek unity we must each look to God together. Each. Look to God. Together.

Unity results from the characteristics that Paul describes as "fruit of the Spirit." Paul used a bunch of words trying to describe the fruit, but the singular verb "is" suggests that it is but one fruit. It is the product of our relationship with God through the indwelling Holy Spirit and it reveals itself through our relationships with each other. Fruit of the Spirit is relational. Unity results from the fruit revealing itself.

God's holy word says,

> By contrast, the fruit of the Spirit is love, joy, peace, patience, kindness, generosity, faithfulness, gentleness, and self-control. There is no law against such things. And those who belong to Christ Jesus have crucified the flesh with its passions and desires. If we live by the Spirit,

let us also be guided by the Spirit. Let us not become conceited, competing against one another, envying one another. Galatians 5:22-26 (NRSV)

The attributes caused by the indwelling of the Holy Spirit – love, joy, peace, patience, kindness, generosity, faithfulness, gentleness and self-control – are individual characteristics revealed through relationship. Unity is the result of the fruit.

When individuals commune with the Holy Spirit in such a way that the fruit of the Holy Spirit is exhibited through them, and they gather together allowing the fruit of the Holy Spirit to influence their interaction, we find unity. The attributes used to describe the fruit are individual traits influencing the world. How can you love without other people to love? How can you be kind without other people to show kindness to? The Holy Spirit urges us to move beyond ourselves and to allow Him, through us, to influence the world around us.

Paul says the opposite is also true. The traits that he calls acts of the flesh are also individual traits revealing themselves through interaction with other people. Please look back to Galatians 5:19. Paul writes:

Now the works of the flesh are obvious: fornication, impurity, licentiousness, idolatry, sorcery, enmities, strife, jealousy, anger, quarrels, dissensions, factions, envy, drunkenness, carousing and things like these. Galatians 5:19-21 (NRSV)

The NIV version uses the word "discord" which is interesting, particularly in light of the Wall Street Journal article declaring that we live in the "age of discord."[xvii] But while the Wall Street Journal seems to believe the age of discord started about a decade ago, Scripture tells us it started in the Garden of Eden. Discord is the way of the world, the way of the flesh.

Paul relates unity with the Holy Spirit and discord with the flesh, the world in which we live. Unity is of God. Discord is of the world.

May you continue seeking God, may the Holy Spirit flow through you, may you exhibit fruit of the Holy Spirit as you live out in the world.

Syrian – Israeli border

THOUGHTS TO CONSIDER

1. Consider influences in your life. Think about the people, places and entertainment that influence your attitude. I recall the season of Lori's radiation treatments. She did not have much energy and she was sensitive to light, so she watched a lot of the television show, The Good Wife. When I was home I watched it with her. It is a drama based on a law firm

and lawsuits, and it is filled with people arguing with one another. It quickly sucked me in, and after watching it for a while, I noticed myself becoming more argumentative. By surrounding myself with a bunch of arguing attorneys on TV, my attitude was influenced.

When I watch shows on news stations where everyone on the show shouts at each other, their arguing influences my attitude. If I spend the same time watching happy things, like comedy or sports when my team wins, my attitude is influenced. And if I spend time reading Scripture, or books about Scripture, or if I spend time in prayer, my attitude is influenced. Pay attention to the things that you allow to influence you. Try to limit the negative influencers and try to spend more time with God.

2. Connect with other people in prayer. This is essential to the Christian walk. We need to spend time alone with God in prayer, but we also need to spend time together, with God in prayer. This is the key to building unity. When we take off our masks and reach out to God together, we create deep, lasting bonds of friendship. Find a group of people you can pray with and take the brave, bold step of praying with them.

3. Act within your sphere of influence. We each have a different sphere but each of us can do something. Allow God's Holy Presence to flow through you and influence people around you. Your position may provide the opportunity to influence people around the globe. Recognize opportunities

and use them for God's glory. Your mobility may be limited, restricting you to your bed or home. Your sphere of influence might be the caregivers you interact with each day, or the people you can write letters or emails to. No matter what your situation is, God gives opportunities each day to allow His glory to shine through you, to be a positive influence on your sphere of influence, to be a beacon of light, to be an agent of love in the world.

4. What are we to do with all this? Unity with God and with each other is so important that Jesus prayed for it as one of His final acts before being arrested. Unity – with God and each other – is central to the Great Commandment. Unity is exhibited through fruit of the Spirit. But we live in a world filled with evil. We live in a world with so much violence. We live in what has been described as "the age of discord." Voices around the globe call out for unity. What will you do?

24

SERVICE BEGETS WHOLENESS

IT WAS [CHRIST] WHO GAVE SOME TO BE APOSTLES, SOME TO BE PROPHETS, SOME TO BE EVANGELISTS, AND SOME TO BE PASTORS AND TEACHERS, TO PREPARE GOD'S PEOPLE FOR WORKS OF SERVICE, SO THAT THE BODY OF CHRIST MAY BE BUILT UP UNTIL WE ALL REACH UNITY IN THE FAITH AND IN THE KNOWLEDGE OF THE SON OF GOD AND BECOME MATURE, ATTAINING TO THE WHOLE MEASURE OF THE FULLNESS OF CHRIST. EPHESIANS 4:11-13

Jesus designed a system with a goal in mind, and the goal is for us to experience, to know in the depths of our souls His life abundant. Jesus says, "I have come that they may have life and have it to the full" (John 10:10). He came to earth with a multi-faceted plan. He came to teach, to provide an example for life, to conquer death, to provide a path for salvation, and He came offering the full measure of His wholeness, His life abundant.

In passage from Ephesians above, Paul echoes this thought as he writes to believers in Ephesus. He writes to his friends who are children of God, they have the Holy Spirit dwelling within them, they know Jesus, they have accepted Jesus as their personal savior, they have salvation, but Paul urges them to move forward in their faith.

Salvation is huge. Knowing Jesus is huge. It is an amazing gift that we can never deserve. As we muck around this world filled with evil, we desperately need God, and Jesus is the only bridge connecting us with God, so recognizing the awful condition of our lives while separated from God, and finding Jesus and crossing that bridge towards God is huge. It is life changing and awesome beyond words, but it is merely the first step towards the life that Jesus came to earth offering. Jesus came offering so much more. He came that we might have life abundant, life with the full measure of His love, His transformative holy presence, His wholeness within us. So accept the gift of salvation, but don't stop there. Open the gift and enjoy it now.

Paul writes a great deal about the transformation of our spirits and souls that is available through Jesus Christ. He urges us to allow total transformation to occur and in the passage above, Paul provides one of the formulas for attaining it. He describes the system whereby pastors, teachers and others are called "to *prepare God's people* for *works of service*, so that the body of Christ may be built up until we all reach *unity* in the faith and in the knowledge of the Son of God and become mature, attaining to the *whole measure of the fullness of Christ.*"

Pastors and teachers are called to equip God's people for works of service. Who are called to service? His people. The moment we first believe we gain the indwelling Holy Spirit, we are adopted as children of God, we become His people. And as His people, we are called to "works of service."

If we stop there, this sounds like an awful deal for us. I have heard our call to service and support described as being analogous to a cult, and I have been asked, "So, if I become a follower of Christ, you suddenly want me to radically change my life, you want me to start giving you my money, and you want me to start working for free. Why would I possibly want to do that?"

If we stop reading the passage after the words, "to equip his people for works of service" we might have a hard time formulating an acceptable answer. At first glance it might seem as if we are being asked to give up much more than we could possibly receive in return. We are being asked to give up some of our most precious resources here on earth – our time and our energy – and for what? Why would a person possibly do that?

Paul continues by explaining that we receive unity, we build relationships with other people that can only be built through love, and we receive "the whole measure of the fullness in Christ" in return. We receive so much more than we could possibly give. We are called to serve for God's purposes, which include our personal growth and unity within the Body of Christ. When we follow God's call to serve others, we grow; we receive immeasurable benefit; we experience the joy, the wholeness, the life abundant that is only available through giving oneself in loving service; God fills us with Him.

Time and time again I hear comments that support and reveal this concept. I have talked with folks after a Kairos weekend ministering to inmates, after they taught a Bible study at the county jail, after they served at the Soup Bowl, after they travelled to far away places offering loving service to others, and time and time again I hear something along the lines of, "I went there to help others, and I received so much more than I gave."

When we offer ourselves in loving service, we build unity within the Body of Christ, we build relationships with people that can be built no other way, and we grow, or it may be more accurate to say, God's holy presence and His life abundant within us grows.

May God enlighten the eyes of our spirit, may you see the opportunities He places in your path, and may He fill you with His courage, strength, wisdom and passion as you take the bold step forward in faith.

THOUGHTS TO CONSIDER

1. Read Ephesians 3:14-21. Paul prays for the people reading his letter. How many times do you see words like strength and power? How does Paul describe Christ filling us with His glory? Meditate on Paul's prayer today. Make it your prayer this week.

2. Read Ephesians 4. How does Paul's prayer introduce the concepts presented in chapter 4? In what specific ways do God's strength and power, His love and His fullness relate to one another?

3. Read John 10:1-21. Jesus says He is the gate and the good shepherd. He also says shepherds lead their sheep out and sheep belonging to the shepherd follow his voice. If Jesus is your shepherd, where is He leading you?

4. Describe the ways Jesus' statements in John 10 and Paul's statements in Ephesians 3 and 4 describe similar concepts.

25

PREPARED FOR SERVICE

THE END OF ALL THINGS IS NEAR. THEREFORE BE CLEAR MINDED AND SELF-CONTROLLED SO THAT YOU CAN PRAY. ABOVE ALL, LOVE EACH OTHER DEEPLY, BECAUSE LOVE COVERS OVER A MULTITUDE OF SINS. OFFER HOSPITALITY TO ONE ANOTHER WITHOUT GRUMBLING. EACH ONE SHOULD USE WHATEVER GIFT HE HAS RECEIVED TO SERVE OTHERS, FAITHFULLY ADMINISTERING GOD'S GRACE IN ITS VARIOUS FORMS. 1 PETER 4:7-10

IT WAS [CHRIST] WHO GAVE SOME TO BE APOSTLES, SOME TO BE PROPHETS, SOME TO BE EVANGELISTS, AND SOME TO BE PASTORS AND TEACHERS, TO PREPARE GOD'S PEOPLE FOR WORKS OF SERVICE, SO THAT THE BODY OF CHRIST MAY BE BUILT UP UNTIL WE ALL REACH UNITY IN THE FAITH AND IN THE KNOWLEDGE OF THE SON OF GOD AND BECOME MATURE, ATTAINING TO THE WHOLE MEASURE OF THE FULLNESS OF CHRIST. EPHESIANS 4:11-13

Scripture is packed with passages urging us to serve God by offering loving service to others, not as a matter of legalism, rather by allowing God's holy love and grace to flow through us. Shortly before writing the passage above Paul wrote, "For we are God's workmanship, created in Christ Jesus to do good works ..." (Ephesians 2:10). Peter wrote, "Each one should use whatever gift he has received to serve others..." (1 Peter 4:10). Jesus reveals the same thought over and over in many different ways. As one of His many statements on the topic He says, "If anyone who wants to be first, he must be the very last, and the servant of all" (Mark 9:35). As followers of Christ who embody His love, offering loving service to others should be the natural response to His indwelling.

While there can be no doubt that He calls us to serve, He does much more than merely call, He also prepares us for the task ahead. He does not send us out as servants unprepared; He equips us for His call. Paul explains that God places people in our path to help us get ready to serve: He calls pastors and teachers to "prepare God's people for works of service." Two questions come to mind: how and why?

First, how do we become prepared? What does it look like? I think it really boils down to (i) studying and meditating on God's word, learning His word, gaining soulful knowledge from Him, and (ii) prayer. It involves prayer for His holy transformation to occur in each of our lives, praying for intercession on behalf of others, and simply praising and thanking God. Through Scripture and prayer we are transformed and equipped to serve. God calls pastors and teachers to help us along the path leading to Him, to help us understand His word, to help us receive His word in our souls, and to help us lead prayerful lives.

We study and meditate on Scripture. We pray. We serve. As I think about it, I see a circle, a cycle ever turning and ever growing. Study, pray and serve. Study, pray and serve. Study, pray and serve. But the individual steps are not necessarily separate. They become blended, and there is really no standard starting point. We start where we are. We may start by serving, we may start by studying, we may start by praying. Wherever we start, the path includes all three facets.

God's holy word is transformative and as we study we are transformed. Prayer connects us with God and as our relationship with the Holy One grows we are transformed. Our eyes are opened to see opportunities before us to serve, and our mind is transformed so we see other people as beings created in God's image who God loves and who are worthy of our love, and we have the desire to serve, which transforms us. The concepts of service, study and prayer become meshed with one another, they become inseparable, they become interwoven as one, they become united.

Memorial built above a 1st Century dwelling venerated by Byzantines as Saint Peter's house in Capernaum, Israel

But why? The passage above suggests that loving service accomplishes three goals. We are prepared for loving service "so that ... we all reach unity ... and become mature, attaining to the whole measure of the fullness of Christ." Certainly loving service helps the people served. It also unites the person serving and the person served, and as this is repeated around the globe unity grows within the broader Body of Christ. Further, people who serve mature in faith, ultimately gaining the "whole measure of the fullness of Christ." This is the life abundant that Jesus Christ promises (see John 10:10).

I understand the message, but I struggle to move from the abstract to the concrete. For example, it is easy to say, "I love God and I love my neighbor" and in the abstract I really believe that I do. But I discover difficulty as the words and abstract thought force me to make radical changes, even when the changes are to something small like the schedule I organized for the day. I imagine driving to a meeting, or whatever the next item on my to-do list for the day may be, and I notice someone along the way who needs help. Do I stop? Do I alter my schedule to act with loving compassion? Or do I pretend not to see so I can continue on with *my* plans for the day?

In the concrete world as I have scheduled it, is there really room for God's plan to reveal itself? Loving my neighbor is pretty easy in the abstract, but in the real world, where the act of loving service may interfere with my plans, where God's call may interfere with my design for my life, where the neighbor may be someone who I fear or dislike, the command becomes a little more difficult.

Whose day is it? Is it a day God created for the revelation of His glory, or is it just another day during which I seek to satisfy my plans and gain pleasure for myself?

We are called to serve and we are continuously being equipped to serve. May your eyes be opened to see the opportunities before you, may you have God's strength, courage and wisdom to step out in faith, may you achieve the goals of His plan for you today, may you build bonds of fellowship with people you encounter, and may you attain the whole measure of the fullness of Jesus Christ.

THOUGHTS TO CONSIDER

1. Read Ephesians 2. Paul describes life before meeting Christ Jesus and life after receiving His redemption. At verse 2:10 he writes that we are "created in Christ Jesus to do good works." Think about your experiences. Describe how you have been driven to serve others since receiving the new life available through Christ Jesus.

2. Read 1 Peter 4. Peter discusses life before and after receiving the redemption available through Christ Jesus. He then writes, "Above all, love each other deeply, because love covers over a multitude of sins" (1 Peter 4:8). How do you see redemption offered through Christ Jesus connected with love? How does His love reveal itself through you?

3. As Peter discusses redemption and service, he throws in the statement, "so that you can pray" (see 1 Peter 4:7). How is your prayer life connected to your life of service? Please list specific examples.

4. Read Matthew 20:24-28. In light of the passages referenced above, how do you interpret Jesus' statement to the disciples? How might you apply His statement to your life? What specific steps will you take this week?

26

From Suffering to Glory

NOW IF WE ARE CHILDREN, THEN WE ARE HEIRS —
HEIRS OF GOD AND CO-HEIRS WITH CHRIST, IF INDEED
WE SHARE IN HIS SUFFERINGS IN ORDER THAT WE MAY
ALSO SHARE IN HIS GLORY. I CONSIDER THAT OUR
PRESENT SUFFERINGS ARE NOT WORTH COMPARING
WITH THE GLORY THAT WILL BE REVEALED TO US."
ROMANS 8:17-18

Over the past week, I have had the opportunity to talk with many people who are in pain. Some suffer physically, others suffer emotional wounds, others suffer spiritual attack, and many suffer some combination of them all.

Most of us have, to some extent, felt physical pain, experienced emotional wounds caused by rejection, ridicule or being abandoned by people we love, known temptation, and known far greater suffering caused by yielding to it. While pain and suffering seem to be part of the human experience, Scripture and experience force me to believe that God flips the script of our suffering to reveal His glory in His perfect time.

Perhaps my eyes were more attuned to suffering last week than usual because I was reading the accounts of Passion Week set forth in the gospels and I was once again reminded of the suffering that Jesus experienced. He was betrayed by a friend, abandoned by His closest friends, rejected by the crowds who had once adored Him, sentenced to execution by a ruler who knew He was innocent, physically tortured, mocked, insulted

1st Century steps leading to Caiaphas' Palace, Jerusalem, Israel

and ridiculed, and ultimately executed by crucifixion. God sat back in silence and allowed it all to occur until, shortly before Jesus breathed His last breath, God reached into our realm and revealed His holy presence. He allowed Jesus to suffer and He refused to punish the people who caused His suffering, but ultimately God reached into our realm announcing His presence, His power, and His authority, and revealing His glory to all who have eyes to see. At noon shortly before Jesus died, the sun stopped shining and darkness fell over Jerusalem, and as Jesus took His last breath, the temple curtain sealing the Holy of Holies was torn in two, an earthquake shook Jerusalem, splitting rocks and opening tombs, and many holy people were raised from the dead (see Matthew 27:45 & 51-53). And then, after a time, Jesus escaped the tomb.

In God's time, He revealed His glory to everyone who has eyes to see. While He allowed suffering, He flipped the script and revealed His glory, all in His time. It is God's miraculous ability to reveal His glory through horrific situations that leads us to deem the day Jesus was crucified as Good Friday. Throughout Scripture we see evidence of God's people suffering, of God allowing suffering for a time, and then of God revealing His glory through the situation. And so it is with us.

Paul wrote, "I consider that our present sufferings are not worth comparing with the glory that will be revealed to us" (Romans 8:18). No matter what you are experiencing, please know and trust that Jesus Christ is with you, He loves you, He understands the pain you feel, and God will reveal His glory through the situation in His perfect time.

THOUGHTS TO CONSIDER

1.   Read Hebrews 4. Jesus promises that we are able to enter His rest through faith. He is our high priest who knows what we are going through.   "Let us then approach the throne of grace with confidence, so that we may receive mercy and find grace to help us in our time of need" (Hebrews 4:16).   How do the promises set forth in God's holy word help you in your time of suffering?

2.   Read Matthew 11:20-30.   Jesus begins the discourse by reprimanding towns that experienced His signs, wonders and miracles, yet who failed to repent.   He then declares that He has infinite power and authority by announcing, "All things have been committed to me by my Father" (Matthew 11:27), and concludes promising His rest to people who take His yoke.   All things are committed to Him, He has all power and authority, and He promises His rest.   How does this promise influence you in your time of suffering?

3.   Read Romans 8.   What does Paul say about suffering in the chapter?   How do his statements influence your view of suffering?

27

FROM SUFFERING TO GLORY – PART II

MY GOD, MY GOD, WHY HAVE YOU FORSAKEN ME? WHY ARE YOU SO FAR FROM SAVING ME, SO FAR FROM THE WORDS OF MY GROANING? OH MY GOD, I CRY OUT BY DAY, BUT YOU DO NOT ANSWER, BY NIGHT, AND AM NOT SILENT.... FROM YOU COMES THE THEME OF MY PRAISE IN THE GREAT ASSEMBLY; BEFORE THOSE WHO FEAR YOU WILL I FULFILL MY VOWS. THE POOR WILL EAT AND BE SATISFIED; THEY WHO SEEK THE LORD WILL PRAISE HIM – MAY YOUR HEARTS LIVE FOREVER! ALL THE ENDS OF THE EARTH WILL REMEMBER AND TURN TO THE LORD, AND ALL THE FAMILIES OF THE NATIONS WILL BOW DOWN BEFORE HIM, FOR DOMINION BELONGS TO THE LORD AND HE RULES OVER THE NATIONS. PSALM 22:1-2 AND 25-28

The psalm is attributed to David. Scripture tells us that God blessed David in amazing ways. Like most of us, he was not perfect and he made some bad decisions, but David trusted God, he knew God, he believed and believed in God, and at times he suffered. In his anguish he felt distant from God; nonetheless, he prayed, trusted that God heard his prayer, and eventually his suffering led to joy.

Jesus, the perfect One, also suffered and He quoted David just before breathing His last breath on the cross saying, "My

God, my God, why have you forsaken me?" (Matthew 27:46). If God allowed David to suffer and if God allowed Jesus to suffer, why am I surprised when I suffer?

Time and time again in Scripture we see God allowing people suffer before flipping the script and revealing His glory through the situation. Think of the Exodus. While in captivity in Egypt, Israelites cried out. God heard their cries, He was concerned about their suffering (see Exodus 3:7), and He saved them in a way that revealed His glory – He parted the sea and they walked across on dry ground (see Exodus 14:22). Suffering led to miraculous deliverance, which revealed God's glory and became the seminal event in their history.

Suffering leads to God revealing His glory in miraculous ways. Think of Job, a righteous man of God who suffered in horrific ways. He lost his wealth, his children were killed, and his body was attacked by disease. As he suffered, God was silent. After a time, God spoke reminding Job of who God is. Eventually, in His perfect time, God revealed His glory and Job realized that he had matured spiritually during the process. At the beginning of the story, Scripture describes Job as righteous, but at the end we see that his faith has matured and his holiness has grown when Job says to God, "My ears had heard of you but now my eyes have seen you" (Job 42:5). Job's suffering positioned him to see God in a new and refreshed way, allowed him to grow spiritually in a way that tranquil prosperity never could, and miraculously revealed God's glory.

While David begins by asking, "My God, my God, why have you forsaken me? Why are you so far from saving me, so far from the words of my groaning?" (Psalm 22:1), he concludes by praising God for His faithfulness (see Psalm 22:22-31). His anguish led him to new joy.

In your season of anguish, please know that God is with you, He is love and He loves you. Never cease crying out to Him because He hears your prayer, and know that in His perfect time in His perfect way, He will reveal His glory. May God comfort you, fill you with His peace, and give you rest.

Possible location of Golgotha, Jerusalem, Israel

THOUGHTS TO CONSIDER

1. Read Exodus 3:1-12. God explains that He hears the cries of His people, knows their suffering and will deliver them from the place suffering to a land flowing with milk and honey. How do you relate God's promise to your life?

2. Read Exodus 14. God delivered His people from Egypt but they were chased by forces from their old life, and they came to a place with no visible escape. Rather than surrendering and returning to their old life, Moses cried out to God for help and God

miraculously delivered them once again. How is God delivering you from your suffering? Do you believe that He hears your prayers?

3. Read Job 10 and 42:1-6. Chapter 10 is part of Job's long lament. He cries out to God. He feels separated from God. In chapter 42 we see Job humbled, satisfied and restored. How do see your suffering in light of the Book of Job?

4. What common threads do you see in Psalm 22, Exodus and Job?

Garden Tomb, possible location of Jesus' burial, Jerusalem, Israel

28

FROM SUFFERING TO GLORY – PART III

THE APOSTLES LEFT THE SANHEDRIN, REJOICING BECAUSE THEY HAD BEEN COUNTED WORTHY OF SUFFERING DISGRACE FOR THE NAME. DAY AFTER DAY, IN THE TEMPLE COURTS AND FROM HOUSE TO HOUSE, THEY NEVER STOPPED TEACHING AND PROCLAIMING THE GOOD NEWS THAT JESUS IS THE CHRIST. ACTS 5:41-42

Portions of the Old Testament suggest that people saw health and wealth as signs of God's blessing and suffering as an indication of God's judgment. But Scripture reveals a monumental shift in how people perceived and responded to suffering after Jesus suffered and left the tomb. Suddenly, suffering for Christ was a sign of holiness, an indication of worthiness and something to be desired.

Shortly after Jesus ascended to heaven, Peter and the apostles were arrested, presented to the Sanhedrin and flogged for the crime of preaching the Gospel. They responded by "rejoicing because they had been counted worthy of suffering disgrace for the Name" (Acts 5:41). They rejoiced because they were worthy of suffering for Christ, and they wore suffering as a badge of honor.

As part of Paul's conversion, God spoke to Ananias, a believer in Damascus, asking him to welcome, pastor and guide Paul to receive the Holy Spirit. God also said, referring to Paul,

"I will show him how much he must suffer for my name" (Acts 9:16). Suffering was not evidence of God's curse or distance; rather it was evidence of holiness encountering an evil world.

Chapel of the Ascension, Mount of Olives, Jerusalem, Israel

It seems to be this sentiment that led Paul to boast about his suffering, writing:

> I have worked much harder, been in prison more frequently, been flogged more severely, and been exposed to death again and again. Five times I received from the Jews the forty lashes minus one. Three times I was beaten with rods, once I was pelted with stones, three

times I was shipwrecked, I spent a night and a day in the open sea, I have been constantly on the move. I have been in danger from rivers, in danger from bandits, in danger from my fellow Jews, in danger from Gentiles; in danger in the city, in danger in the country, in danger at sea; and in danger from false believers. I have labored and toiled and have often gone without sleep; I have known hunger and thirst and have often gone without food; I have been cold and naked. Besides everything else, I face daily the pressure of my concern for all the churches. Who is weak, and I do not feel weak? Who is led into sin, and I do not inwardly burn? If I must boast, I will boast of the things that show my weakness. 2 Corinthians 11:23-30

Paul was certainly a man of God. He was holy. He was filled with the Holy Spirit. God healed people response to Paul's prayers. Paul followed God's calling. He was one of, if not the, greatest evangelist of all time, yet God allowed him to suffer. When God allowed Jesus to suffer, He ultimately revealed His glory through the events. When God allowed Paul, Peter and the apostles to suffer, He ultimately revealed His glory through each situation. The same is true of our suffering.

How are you suffering for Christ? Paul wrote, "I consider that our present sufferings are not worth comparing with the glory that will be revealed to us" (Romans 8:18). No matter what you are experiencing, please know and trust that Jesus Christ is with you, He loves you, He understands the pain you feel, and God will reveal His glory through the situation in His perfect time.

THOUGHTS TO CONSIDER

1. Read Acts 3-5. Shortly after Jesus' arrest, torture, crucifixion and resurrection, Peter, John and other apostles appear in the vicinity of Jesus' suffering and they heal, preach, are arrested and miraculously released before repeating the cycle. God reveals His glory through them in miraculous ways and then He allows them to suffer imprisonment. How does the cycle of their ministry influence your view of your suffering?

2. Read Acts 9. Saul meets Jesus and is converted. As he begins preaching the good news of Jesus Christ, "the Jews conspired to kill him" (Acts 9:23), and he turned and preached to Hellenists and "they tried to kill him" (Acts 9:30). As God prepared Saul (aka Paul) for ministry, God promised Saul that he would suffer for God (see Acts 9:16) and Saul's life was in constant danger from all sides.

3. Read 2 Corinthians 11. How do Paul's experiences influence your view of suffering?

29

FROM SUFFERING TO GLORY – PART IV

AS HE WENT ALONG, HE SAW A MAN BLIND FROM BIRTH. HIS DISCIPLES ASKED HIM, "RABBI, WHO SINNED, THIS MAN OR HIS PARENTS, THAT HE WAS BORN BLIND?" "NEITHER THIS MAN NOR HIS PARENTS SINNED," SAID JESUS, "BUT THIS HAPPENED SO THAT THE WORKS OF GOD MIGHT BE DISPLAYED IN HIS LIFE." JOHN 9:1-3

Cathedral of Saint Anne, Jerusalem, Israel

In our own unique way, at times we each encounter anguish. It is a part of the human experience. I have heard folks discuss the storms, tribulation, pain and chaos we each encounter along our path. As the metaphors demonstrate, the lens through which we view suffering shapes our experience.

While reminding his friends to expect suffering, Paul mentions the counterintuitive concept of rejoicing in it. To the church in Philippi Paul wrote, "For it has been granted to you on behalf of Christ not only to believe in him, but also to suffer for him…" (Philippians 1:29), and to the Colossians, "Now I rejoice in what was suffered for you…" (Colossians 1:24), and he urges Timothy to "join me in suffering for the gospel, by the power of God" (2 Timothy 1:8) and to "endure hardship with us like a good soldier of Christ Jesus" (2 Timothy 2:3), and he praised the church of Thessalonica for growing in faith while enduring pain, suffering and turmoil (see 1 Thessalonians 1:6 and 2 Thessalonians 1:5).

The words written to Timothy suggest that for Paul, suffering was something to join in, boast about and rejoice in. It was a badge of honor, a sign of dedication to Christ, an indication of holiness, the expected result from holiness encountering the sinful world. Certainly, the message Paul preached led to a great deal of his suffering. Had he simply stopped preaching the Gospel, the beatings and threats would have ended, nonetheless he continued preaching with urgency. He simply could not stop telling others about the good news of Jesus Christ, he rejoiced in the honor of sharing Christ's suffering, and God continues to reveal His glory through him.

God also reveals His glory through the suffering of regular folks like us who are merely making our way through life. Scripture tells of a man who was born blind. Discussing the man's physical condition, Jesus explains, "this happened so that the works of God might be displayed in his life" (John 9:3). God allowed the man to suffer for a time so that His glory might be revealed. Similarly, God allowed Lazarus, Martha and Mary to suffer through his sickness, death and burial, all so that, in God's time, Lazarus might be raised from the dead and God's glory might be revealed (see John 11). Scripture records many other miraculous healing stories revealing similar displays of God glory – in each, God allowed people to suffer for a time before demonstrating His mercy, love, authority and unimaginable power through them. Time and time again, suffering leads to the revelation of God's glory.

Scripture also explains two additional positive consequences of troubles: they cause us to rely on God and they allow us to see the power of prayer. As Paul wrote to the church in Corinth he mentioned the extreme troubles he faced in Asia, comparing the situation to a death sentence. He continued writing, "But this happened that we might not rely on ourselves but on God, who raises the dead. He has delivered us from such a deadly peril, and he will deliver us. On him we have set our hope that he will continue to deliver us, as you help us by your prayers. Then many will give thanks on our behalf for the gracious favor granted us in the answer to the prayers of many" (2 Corinthians 1:9-11).

What storm is blowing in your life? Praise God. Trust in God. Thank God. Rely on God. Ask others to pray for you. He has delivered you before and He will deliver you again. May God continue to reveal His glory through you in His perfect time.

Pool of Bethesda, Jerusalem, Israel

THOUGHTS TO CONSIDER

1.   Read John 9. Jesus healed a man who had been blind his entire life. The disciples asked why the man was born blind. Jesus answered that it happened so that God might reveal His glory through the man (see John 9:3). The man suffered. His parents and family suffered.   God allowed human suffering so that people might experience God through the entire situation. Do you see parallels with your suffering?

2.   Read John 11. Jesus raised Lazarus from the dead, and revealed God's glory by doing so, but He allowed Lazarus and his family and friends to suffer for a long time. How does the account of Lazarus influence your view of suffering and God's glory?

3.   Read John 15. Jesus says, "If the world hates you, keep in mind that it hated me first. If you belonged to the world, it would love you as its own. As it is, you do not belong to the world but I have chosen you out of the world. That is why the world hates you" (John 15:18-19). When connected to the accounts in John 9 & 11, how does this passage influence your view of suffering and God's glory?

Pool of Bethesda, Jerusalem, Israel

30

THE WORD

IN THE BEGINNING WAS THE WORD, AND THE
WORD WAS WITH GOD, AND THE WORD WAS GOD.
HE WAS WITH GOD IN THE BEGINNING. THROUGH
HIM ALL THINGS WERE MADE; WITHOUT HIM NOTHING
WAS MADE THAT HAS BEEN MADE. IN HIM WAS LIFE,
AND THAT LIFE WAS THE LIGHT OF ALL MANKIND. THE
LIGHT SHINES IN THE DARKNESS, AND THE DARKNESS
HAS NOT UNDERSTOOD IT. JOHN 1:1-5

THE WORD BECAME FLESH AND MADE HIS
DWELLING AMONG US. WE HAVE SEEN HIS GLORY,
THE GLORY OF THE ONE AND ONLY, WHO CAME
FROM THE FATHER, FULL OF GRACE AND TRUTH.
JOHN 1:14

"In the beginning was the Word, and the Word was with God, and the Word was God. He was with God in the beginning" (John 1:1-2). John begins his Gospel with these insightful, revealing, poetic words. Twelve verses later he writes, "The Word became flesh and made his dwelling among us" (John 1:14).

The "Word." By using the terminology John refers to the power, mind, essence ... the totality of God. In Aramaic the term translated as "Word" is a circumlocution for the Name of God. For those believing it was inappropriate to utter the Name of the Almighty, the Holy, the Creator, the Word was used as a substituted term referring to Him allowing discussion about Him.

The Greek term for "Word" is logos, the root of logic, which refers to rational thought communicated – the mind of God. The Hebrew term for "Word" refers to God's power. God's Word is powerful. Consider the opening words of Scripture. Like John's Gospel, Genesis begins with the words "In the beginning…." "In the beginning God created the heavens and the earth." And how did God create these things? He spoke. God spoke and there was light. God spoke and earth and water and sky were separated. God spoke and animals, birds and fish came to be. God spoke and people were created. When God speaks, things happen. His Word is unimaginably powerful.

The Word – the mind of God, the power of God, the essence and totality of God, God Himself – became flesh. Jesus has always been and always will be. Jesus was and is God. He does not merely reflect God's Glory, Jesus was and is the Divine, the Holy the Pure. To further explain this thought, Jesus said, "I and the Father are one" (John 10:30). Jesus is God.

While on earth He demonstrated how to live through His actions, He taught, He told us how we should live by giving specific direction on things we should do and things we should not do, He revealed God's glory in miraculous ways, He prayed for us, He suffered and died for us, He ascended to heaven, and He sends the Holy Spirit who lives with us, dwells within us and helps us. Jesus says, "I tell you the truth, anyone who has faith in me will do what I have been doing. He will do even greater things than these, because I am going to the Father… And I will ask the Father, and he will give you another Counselor to be with you forever – the Spirit of truth" (John 14:12-17).

"Anyone who has faith in me will do…" Faith equals doing. If we believe, we act on our belief. Faith, belief and action are inseparable, and Jesus is very specific regarding the sort of action belief inspires saying, "Anyone who has faith in me will do what I have been doing. He will do even greater things …"

Consider a few of the amazing things Scripture tells us that Jesus did. He taught with authority, cast out demons, healed multitudes, controlled the weather, and turned water into wine. He revealed God's glory through word, sign and deed. How can we possibly do the things Jesus did? How can we possibly do greater things than He did?

Through followers of Christ empowered by the Holy Spirit, God reveals the full story of His redemption, life, love and light. We not only have the benefit of the fullness of His story, we have His power dwelling within us – Jesus also says, "But you will receive power when the Holy Spirit comes on you…" (Acts 1:8). The Word has power and He empowers us through the Holy Spirit.

May you know the power, may you experience the power, may you trust the power, may you allow the Holy Spirit to fill you, flow through you, and reveal His love to everyone you encounter.

THOUGHTS TO CONSIDER

1. Read Genesis 1 and 2. What do the creation accounts tell you about God?

2. Read Luke 10:18 and John 8:58. The passages include two of Jesus' statements where He claims to have been living for a long, long time, so long that the statements suggest He is eternal.

3. Read John 10:30. Jesus says, "I and the Father are one." This is a claim of deity.

4. Do His claims of longevity, suggestions of being eternal and claim of deity influence your understanding of who Jesus is? Do they help you to see that He is God?

5. Jesus gave up His heavenly glory for a time to come to earth as a man, so that we might gain His life, His light, His love, and so that we might do the things that Jesus did. If you believe you do the things Jesus did. How does this realization change your to-do list today?

Via Dolorosa, Jerusalem, Israel

31

INSTRUCTIONS FOR LIFE

THEN SOME PHARISEES AND TEACHERS OF THE LAW CAME TO JESUS FROM JERUSALEM AND ASKED, "WHY DO YOUR DISCIPLES BREAK THE TRADITION OF THE ELDERS? THEY DON'T WASH THEIR HANDS BEFORE THEY EAT!"

JESUS REPLIED, "AND WHY DO YOU BREAK THE COMMAND OF GOD FOR THE SAKE OF YOUR TRADITION? FOR GOD SAID, 'HONOR YOUR FATHER AND MOTHER' AND 'ANYONE WHO CURSES HIS FATHER OR MOTHER MUST BE PUT TO DEATH.' BUT YOU SAY THAT IF A MAN SAYS TO HIS FATHER OR MOTHER, 'WHATEVER HELP YOU MIGHT OTHERWISE HAVE RECEIVED FROM ME IS A GIFT DEVOTED TO GOD,' HE IS NOT TO 'HONOR HIS FATHER' WITH IT. THUS YOU NULLIFY THE WORD OF GOD FOR THE SAKE OF YOUR TRADITION. YOU HYPOCRITES! ISAIAH WAS RIGHT WHEN HE PROPHESIED ABOUT YOU:

"THESE PEOPLE HONOR ME WITH THEIR LIPS, BUT THEIR HEARTS ARE FAR FROM ME. THEY WORSHIP ME IN VAIN; THEIR TEACHINGS ARE BUT RULES TAUGHT BY MEN."

JESUS CALLED THE CROWD TO HIM AND SAID, "LISTEN AND UNDERSTAND. WHAT GOES INTO A MAN'S MOUTH DOES NOT MAKE HIM 'UNCLEAN,' BUT WHAT COMES OUT OF HIS MOUTH, THAT IS WHAT MAKES HIM 'UNCLEAN.'" MATTHEW 15:1-11

Saint Catherine's Monastery, Sinai Peninsula, Egypt

Jesus blasted religious leaders for, among other things, their legalism; yet He also issued many commands. Reading the gospels and Book of Acts, I count 121 commands Jesus said to people.[2] It seems that He viewed the legalistic demands of religious leaders of His day as an intricate web of stumbling blocks set up to entrap and ensnare, while viewing His commands as guideposts marking the path to freedom.

At first glance commands, rules and regulations seem to restrict freedom and limit liberty because, by their very nature, they direct us towards certain choices and away from others; however, rules are necessary for liberty. As revealed from video streams showing war-torn regions with buildings reduced to rubble, empty streets, closed shops and people hiding in their homes, chaos restricts freedom while proper rules allow liberty to flourish: they allow a system to exist within which liberty is possible.

A while back I heard Billy Graham discuss this concept. He presented baseball as an analogy concluding that a baseball game without rules would not work. So it is with society and individual life, so long as the rules are appropriate and enforced with love, respect and dignity.

In this light, while Jesus criticizes legalism, He prescribes rules for living. He commands us to preach, teach, speak and tell. He tells us to follow him. He tells us to repent, believe, have faith and pray. He tells us not to do certain things. For instance, He commands not to swear, not to store up treasure on earth, not to worry, not to judge, not to be afraid, among others. He tells us to listen, understand and hear. He tells us to open our eyes and let nothing be wasted and receive the Holy Spirit. He

---

[2] The count excludes commands that Jesus spoke to evil spirits. For instance, when Jesus encountered a man who suffered with a legion of demons within him, Jesus ordered the legion of demons "Come out of this man you impure spirit!" (Mark 5:8). I did not count this or others like it.

tells us to love each other, and to feed [His] lambs and to take care of [His] sheep.

While the instructions are taken from conversations, Jesus explicitly refers to one instruction as a "command." He says, "A new command I give you: Love one another. As I have loved you, so you must love one another. By this all men will know that you are my disciples, if you love one another" (John 13:34-35). He also says, "This is my command: love each other" (John 15:17).

Jesus calls us to treat one another with love, mercy, grace and compassion, which are the keys to rules that avoid legalism. We are not called to act dogmatically, rather, we are called to embody His essence – His love, mercy, grace and compassion – through soulful transformation where we become vessels filled with Him, which instills a desire to follow Him, tell others about Him, focus on Him, love others, etc.

Legalism is intellectual. Following Jesus' instructions for life begins with spiritual transformation. May you allow the love of Jesus Christ to fill you, flow through you and transform the world within your realm of influence.

THOUGHTS TO CONSIDER

1. Read Matthew 5:17-45. After explaining that He has come to fulfill the law, not to abolish it, Jesus calls us to transcend above the law. He calls us to spiritual transformation leading to holiness, which will be revealed through our actions. With this goal in mind, Jesus discusses anger, adultery, divorce, oaths, retaliation and loving enemies. How might you apply this teaching to your life today?

2. Read Matthew 12:1-14. Jesus seems to regularly provoke religious leaders regarding rules relating to the Sabbath, urging them to look beyond the intricacy of rules and to act in ways demonstrating love, compassion and mercy to others. What rules do see around you that serve to block justice, mercy and love? How do you respond to the rules?

3. How do Jesus' commands conform with His call leading us away from legalism?

4. Read Hosea 6. Jesus' teaching was not new when He taught it. God called prophets to urge His people to transcend above the law to lives filled with love and compassion. How does this alter your view of Jesus' teaching?

5. How will you respond?

Michelangelo's Moses, San Pietro in Vincoli, Rome, Italy

32

JESUS WARNS

AS HE TAUGHT, JESUS SAID, "WATCH OUT FOR THE TEACHERS OF THE LAW. THEY LIKE TO WALK AROUND IN FLOWING ROBES AND BE GREETED IN THE MARKETPLACES, AND HAVE THE MOST IMPORTANT SEATS IN THE SYNAGOGUES AND THE PLACES OF HONOR AT BANQUETS. THEY DEVOUR WIDOWS' HOUSES AND FOR A SHOW MAKE LENGTHY PRAYERS. SUCH MEN WILL BE PUNISHED MOST SEVERELY." MARK 12:38-40

GOING A LITTLE FARTHER, HE FELL WITH HIS FACE TO THE GROUND AND PRAYED, "MY FATHER, IF IT IS POSSIBLE, MAY THIS CUP BE TAKEN FROM ME. YET NOT AS I WILL, BUT AS YOU WILL." THEN HE RETURNED TO HIS DISCIPLES AND FOUND THEM SLEEPING. "COULD YOU MEN NOT KEEP WATCH WITH ME FOR ONE HOUR?" HE ASKED PETER. "WATCH AND PRAY SO THAT YOU WILL NOT FALL INTO TEMPTATION. THE SPIRIT IS WILLING, BUT THE BODY IS WEAK." MATTHEW 26:39-41

God came to earth in fully human form. During His brief ministry, Jesus revealed God's glory through His teaching, miracles, compassion, mercy, love and, while we do not often discuss it, His instructions for living. I recently read Scripture focusing on Jesus' commands. Eleven times Jesus instructs people to follow Him. Five times He commands people to love. Twice He orders people to repent, twice He says to believe and seven times He instructs people to pray. Scripture records one command to wash one another's feet.

More often than the other commands, He warns. Jesus commands us to be on guard, to be careful, to watch out and to beware 19 times. Approximately 16% of His commands recorded in Scripture are warnings.

Old City Wall, Jerusalem, Israel

What is He warning us about? What is so important that Jesus, God in physical form, during His brief earthly ministry, took time to warn us about? He warns about pride, arrogance and greed. He warns about becoming trapped by the anxieties of our lives.

He tells us to be on guard against people because people will persecute Christians. He warns about falling into temptation.

The most frequent warning is about deception, specifically about being deceived by inaccurate teaching and false prophets. Jesus warns about our inability to see truth clearly. He knows that we cannot see as clearly as He sees. He knows we are susceptible to being fooled and tricked. He knows that we struggle to discern truth from fiction. And He knows that some people would like to see us fooled.

As part of the Sermon on the Mount Jesus says, "Watch out for false prophets. They come to you in sheep's clothing, but inwardly they are ferocious wolves. By their fruit you will recognize them" (Matthew 7:15-16).

During a conversation between Jesus, Peter, James, John and Andrew on the Mount of Olives Jesus says, "Watch out that no one deceives you" (Mark 13:5).

On another occasion Jesus travelled to the eastern shore of the Sea of Galilee. Matthew describes a conversation between Jesus and the disciples writing, "Be careful," Jesus said to them. "Be on your guard against the yeast of the Pharisees and Sadducees" (Matthew 16:6). A few verses later, Matthew explains the disciples understood Jesus was talking about their teaching.

Mark writes, "As he taught, Jesus said, 'Watch out for the teachers of the law. They like to walk around in flowing robes and be greeted in the marketplaces, and have the most important seats in the synagogues and the places of honor at banquets. They devour widows' houses and for a show make lengthy prayers. Such men will be punished most severely'" (Mark 12:38-40). The warning has to do with pride and arrogance, and the impact that a teacher's character has on his or her teaching.

Watch out. Be careful. Be on guard. Beware. Jesus warns about deception, about inaccurate teaching and about false prophesy.

New Gate, Jerusalem, Israel

What are we to do? We need to hear the warning and recognize we are at risk, and we need to mitigate the risk by studying, meditating on and understanding God's word. After listening to someone teach about God's holy word, we need to go to Scripture, study it, examine it and verify that the teaching conforms with God's word. We need to act like the folks Paul and Silas met in Berea. As Paul and Silas taught the people there "received the message with great eagerness and examined the Scriptures every day to see if what Paul said was true" (Acts 17:11). After listeners heard his message, they turned to Scripture to verify the accuracy of his teaching.

This is how we should respond. Appreciating that we are unable to see clearly, we must, more so than ever, test what we hear. We must verify the messages we hear conform to Scripture. Of equal importance, we must continuously pray for God's discerning Spirit to guide us. While we cannot see as clearly as God sees, He has given us minds and the ability to think. Use the talents God has given you, along with your experience, built on the foundation of Scripture and prayer.

May God fill you with His wisdom, with His discerning Spirit, with His understanding, with His strength, power and boldness. May He provide clear assurance that He is truly with you. May He continue to reveal His glory through you.

Israeli Wall, Bethlehem, West Bank

Thoughts to Consider

1.   Read Matthew 6:1-4. Jesus tells us to "be careful not to do your 'acts of righteousness' before men, to be seen by them."   Then He describes what He means with an example. Can you think of times in your life when you might have done good things for the wrong reasons? If you are being "careful not to do" that, what might you have done differently in those instances?

2. Read Matthew 10:17-42.   Jesus begins the discourse regarding persecution saying, "Be on your guard against men; they will hand you over to the local councils and flog you in their synagogues." He continues saying, "All men will hate you because of me..." (v.22) and more. After reading the entire discourse, have you experienced separation from the world because of Jesus? How so? How have you needed to "Be on guard against men"?

3.   Read Matthew 24:1-25. Jesus left the temple and walked to the Mount of Olives where He sat and taught. The disciples asked Him when the end of the age would come and what signs would foretell it. Jesus answered, "Watch out that no one deceives you. For many will come in my name, claiming, 'I am the Christ' and will deceive many" (v.4-5). What teaching do you believe creates deception today? What causes you to believe it is deceptive as opposed to God's truth?

4.   Are you surprised to hear that the most common category of Jesus' commands is warnings and the

most common warning is against deception? How do you respond? What steps will you take to guard against being deceived?

Cathedral of the Annunciation, Nazareth, Israel

33

APOSTLES WARN

BE SELF-CONTROLLED AND ALERT. YOUR ENEMY THE DEVIL PROWLS AROUND LIKE A ROARING LION LOOKING FOR SOMEONE TO DEVOUR. RESIST HIM, STANDING FIRM IN THE FAITH, BECAUSE YOU KNOW THAT YOUR BROTHERS THROUGHOUT THE WORLD ARE UNDERGOING THE SAME KIND OF SUFFERINGS. 1 PETER 5:8-9

FOR SUCH MEN ARE FALSE APOSTLES, DECEITFUL WORKMEN, MASQUERADING AS APOSTLES OF CHRIST. AND NO WONDER, FOR SATAN HIMSELF MASQUERADES AS AN ANGEL OF LIGHT. IT IS NOT SURPRISING, THEN, IF HIS SERVANTS MASQUERADE AS SERVANTS OF RIGHTEOUSNESS. THEIR END WILL BE WHAT THEIR ACTIONS DESERVE. 2 CORINTHIANS 11:13-15

DEAR CHILDREN, THIS IS THE LAST HOUR; AND AS YOU HAVE HEARD THAT THE ANTICHRIST IS COMING, EVEN NOW MANY ANTICHRISTS HAVE COME. THIS IS HOW WE KNOW IT IS THE LAST HOUR. THEY WENT OUT FROM US, BUT THEY DID NOT REALLY BELONG TO US. FOR IF THEY HAD BELONGED TO US, THEY WOULD HAVE REMAINED WITH US; BUT THEIR GOING SHOWED THAT NONE OF THEM BELONGED TO US. ... I AM WRITING THESE THINGS TO YOU ABOUT THOSE WHO ARE TRYING TO LEAD YOU ASTRAY. AS FOR YOU, THE ANOINTING YOU RECEIVED FROM HIM REMAINS IN YOU, AND YOU DO NOT NEED ANYONE TO TEACH YOU. BUT AS HIS ANOINTING TEACHES YOU

Randy L. Allen

ABOUT ALL THINGS AND AS THAT ANOINTING IS REAL, NOT
COUNTERFEIT – JUST AS IT HAS TAUGHT YOU, REMAIN IN
HIM. 1 JOHN 2:18-19 & 26-27

Gloria in Excelsis Deo Chapel, Bethlehem, West Bank

During His brief ministry on earth, Jesus gave lots of warnings. Time and time again he urged folks to watch out, beware, be on guard, and be careful. His most frequent warning was about distortions of truth. He urges us to watch out, be careful, be on guard, and beware of deceptive and inaccurate teaching. The apostles convey similar warnings. They describe Satan prowling and people within the church influenced by evil forces seeking to deceive. They urge us to keep watch and to be alert.

As Paul concluded what would be his last journey through Asia Minor, he asked the leaders of the church in Ephesus to meet him in Miletus. Explaining that the Holy Spirit had made it clear he would soon be imprisoned, Paul told them that they would not see each other again. He was saying farewell to his friends. He did not have much time because the boat to Caesarea was preparing to leave, and he wanted to be on it so he could be in Jerusalem for Pentecost.

As he said goodbye, Paul spoke with urgency saying,

> "Keep watch over yourselves and all the flock of which the Holy Spirit has made you overseers. Be shepherds of the church of God, which he bought with his own blood. I know that after I leave, savage wolves will come in among you and will not spare the flock. Even from your own number men will arise to distort the truth in order to draw away disciples after them. So be on your guard! Remember that for three years I never stopped warning each of you night and day with tears." Acts 20:28-31

Paul's words are very similar to Jesus' words as he warns about distorted truth. "Keep watch ... even from your own number men will arise to distort the truth ... so be on your guard!" It is striking that at this particular time and setting, as their time together expires and he bids his friends farewell, Paul urgently warns about distorted truth in general, and specifically, distortions from within the church.

The warning was central to his farewell message and common in his letters. He urges readers "to watch out for those who cause divisions and put obstacles in your way that are contrary to the teaching you have learned. Keep away from them" (Romans 16:17). He ribs the church in Corinth saying, "For if someone comes to you and preaches a Jesus other than the Jesus we preached ... you put up with it easily enough" (2 Corinthians 11:4). He urges the church in Ephesus to "become mature, attaining to the whole measure of the fullness of Christ. Then we will no longer be infants, tossed back and forth by the waves, and blown here and there by every wind of teaching and by the cunning and craftiness of people in their deceitful scheming" (Ephesians 4:13-14). Paul issues additional warning and instruction to Titus and Timothy (see Titus 1:10-13 and 1 Timothy 4:1-2).

Peter describes Satan prowling like a lion seeking to devour and John describes people within the church who are influenced by a spirit opposed to Jesus Christ and who seek to lead others astray. Jesus and the apostles repeatedly warn about deceptive teaching and distorted truth. The risk exists, but how do we mitigate it?

Last week we discussed mimicking the Bereans by studying Scripture and verifying the messages we hear are consistent with the word of God (see Acts 17:11). Consider also Paul's advice to the Ephesians. Immediately before the passage quoted above, Paul explains that Jesus Christ calls prophets, evangelists, pastors and teachers to equip people for works of service and to build up and unite the body of Christ in faith, understanding and maturity, "attaining the whole measure of the fullness of Christ" (Ephesians 4:13). He continues writing, "Then we will no longer be infants, tossed back and forth by the waves, and blown here and there by every wind of teaching and by the cunning and craftiness of people in their deceitful scheming" (Ephesians 4:14).

Paul urges us to build a strong foundation of faith based on the truth of Jesus Christ. He urges us to grow in maturity of faith and knowledge. He urges us to demonstrate our faith through acts of service, and he envisions unity within the body of Christ with each individual experiencing the fullness of Christ. Study Scripture, pray and serve others. These are the three legs of the stool of faith. Study, pray and serve. Study and meditate on Scripture so you know God's holy word. Pray and gain relationship with Him. And serve others because faith without action is hollow. Study, pray and serve, and grow in maturity on the foundation of truth.

May God enlighten the eyes of your spirit, may He open your ears, may He soften your heart so it is fertile soil allowing His seed to grow.

THOUGHTS TO CONSIDER

1. Read Titus 1 & 2. Paul writes,

> Since an overseer is entrusted with God's work, he must be blameless – not overbearing, not quick-tempered, not given to drunkenness, not violent, not pursuing dishonest gain. Rather, he must be hospitable, one who loves what is good, who is self-controlled, upright, holy and disciplined. He must hold firmly to the trustworthy message as it has been taught, so that he can encourage others by sound doctrine and refute those who oppose it. For there are many rebellious people, mere talkers and deceivers, especially those of the

circumcision group. They must be silenced, because they are ruining whole households by teaching things they ought not teach – and that for the sake of dishonest gain. Titus 1:7-11

After discussing qualities that should characterize church leaders, Paul discusses rebellion and inaccurate teaching within the church and declares, "They must be silenced." If you have been called to serve as a leader within your congregation, what is your daily discipline to stay "self-controlled, upright, holy and disciplined"? How do you identify deceptive teaching? How does your church handle deceptive teaching within it?

2. Read 1 Timothy 4. Paul addresses specific inaccurate teaching within the church at the time he wrote the letter. Paul writes to remind Timothy about the solid doctrine he has been taught and encourages him to stand firm on solid teaching. What parallels do you see in your church today? How do you respond?

3. Read Romans 16. The Book of Romans is a carefully crafted, clearly articulated presentation of the Good News of Jesus Christ. Paul concludes the letter with a warning – he warns, "I urge you, brothers, to watch out for those who cause divisions and put obstacles in your way that are contrary to the teaching you have learned" (Romans 16:17). Then he offers simple advice saying, "Keep away from them" (id). Think back over your life of faith. Who has caused divisions or set up obstacles in your path?

How did you handle them? How will you handle them in the future?

4. Read 1 John 2. John uses different language than Paul. Do you believe John is addressing similar concerns? Why or why not?

Synagogue, Magdala, Israel

34

PAUL'S FAREWELL

"NOW I KNOW THAT NONE OF YOU AMONG WHOM
I HAVE GONE ABOUT PREACHING THE KINGDOM WILL
EVER SEE ME AGAIN. THEREFORE, I DECLARE TO YOU
TODAY THAT I AM INNOCENT OF THE BLOOD OF ALL MEN.
FOR I HAVE NOT HESITATED TO PROCLAIM TO YOU THE
WHOLE WILL OF GOD. KEEP WATCH OVER YOURSELVES
AND ALL THE FLOCK OF WHICH THE HOLY SPIRIT HAS
MADE YOU OVERSEERS. BE SHEPHERDS OF THE CHURCH
OF GOD, WHICH HE BOUGHT WITH HIS OWN BLOOD. I
KNOW THAT AFTER I LEAVE, SAVAGE WOLVES WILL COME
IN AMONG YOU AND WILL NOT SPARE THE FLOCK. EVEN
FROM YOUR OWN NUMBER MEN WILL ARISE TO DISTORT
THE TRUTH IN ORDER TO DRAW AWAY DISCIPLES AFTER
THEM. SO BE ON YOUR GUARD! REMEMBER THAT FOR
THREE YEARS I NEVER STOPPED WARNING EACH OF YOU
NIGHT AND DAY WITH TEARS." ACTS 20:25-31

Paul collected a love offering from the young churches
across what is now Greece and Turkey for the church in
Jerusalem. As he traveled to Jerusalem, he passed near Ephesus.
He did not want to take time to stop in Ephesus, so he invited
friends to meet him in Miletus before he boarded the boat
heading to Caesarea. As Paul traveled, the Holy Spirit told him
that he would soon be imprisoned, so he planned to say goodbye
to his friends.

As he said goodbye, he spoke with urgency saying the passage first quoted above. He declared that this was truly a farewell saying, "none of you … will ever see me again." Following that shocking news, Paul says that he is innocent of their blood. Why does he say that? It is as if he proclaimed that he would not be responsible for their death. Why would he possibly be found guilty or held accountable for their blood or death?

The words refer to Ezekiel 3:17-19. God calls Ezekiel to be a watchman tasked to proclaim God's word as specifically directed. What do watchmen do? They stay in the watchtower, look out for danger and when they see danger coming, they alert the army to get ready. They sound the alarm, ring the bell, alert the people responsible for the army so they will defend the city. If the watchman fails to notice the approaching risk or fails to alert the army, they fail at their job and they will be held responsible for the ensuing destruction. However, if the watchman alerts the army, he did his job, and if the army fails to protect the city, the army will be held accountable.

So God calls Ezekiel to be His watchman. As God's watchman, Ezekiel must identify risk and alert people to it. When God instructs Ezekiel to approach someone and speak God's word, Ezekiel must choose whether to act or whether to abstain. If Ezekiel follows through as called, the person to whom he speaks must decide whether to heed Ezekiel's warning and that person will be responsible for his or her choice. However, if God calls Ezekiel to speak and he chooses not to speak, Ezekiel will be held accountable for the person's blood. Paul is saying that, like Ezekiel, he is a watchman. He is called to alert people to danger, and because he followed through on God's call by speaking the words God gave him to speak, he is innocent of the choices they subsequently make.

Caesarea Maritime, Israel

Paul proclaims that he did the job that God called him to do, and he urges his friends to follow through on their calling. Like the good watchman, Paul urges his friends to keep watch first over themselves and then over their flock. He urges them to be the shepherds that God calls them to be. He urges them to follow through on their task, reminding them that their task starts with personal responsibility, and to beware of people who might deter them saying,

> "Be shepherds of the church of God, which he bought with his own blood. I know that after I leave, savage wolves will come in among you and will not spare the flock. Even from your own number men will arise to distort the truth in order to draw away disciples after them. So be on your guard! Remember that for three years I never stopped warning each of you night and day with tears."

Paul warns his friends that "savage wolves will come in among" them from within their group. Attacks will come from within the church; people inside the church will distort the truth, "So be on your guard!" As shepherds, Paul's friends were tasked with guiding a flock and discerning which members of the flock were actually wolves dressed as sheep.

God calls each of us to serve Him. He called Ezekiel and Paul to be watchmen. He called Paul's friends in Ephesus to shepherd a young church. What is He calling you to do? As part of Paul's farewell speech, he urges his friends to follow through on their calling. May you hear God's call, and when you do, may God fill you with His strength, courage and passion to act. And as you prepare to say farewell, may you, like Paul, know in your heart that you faithfully accomplished each appointed task.

Aqueduct, Caesarea Beach, Israel

THOUGHTS TO CONSIDER

1. Read Matthew 7:15-20. Jesus says false prophets will "come to you in sheep's clothing, but inwardly they are ferocious wolves" (Matthew 7:15). He continues explaining that we are able to recognize them by the fruit they produce. How does this teaching from the Sermon on the Mount compare with Paul's farewell address? How are the different?

2. Read Ezekiel 34. God speaks through the prophet Ezekiel providing very specific instructions for people whom He calls to serve as shepherds. God calls shepherds to strengthen the weak, heal the sick, bind up the injured, search for the lost and bring back strays (see Ezekiel 34:4). How does Ezekiel 34 change your reading of Paul's farewell address?

3. Read Jeremiah 23. Speaking through the prophet Jeremiah, God decries shepherds who scatter His flock (see Jeremiah 23:1), then He describes His heartache over false prophets and priests who mislead His people. He says, "Concerning the prophets: my heart is broken within me; all my bones tremble" (Jeremiah 23:9). Have you ever considered that God's heart might be broken over our decisions? How does that make you feel?

4. Do God's warnings issued through the prophets and through Paul still apply today? How should we apply the warnings in our present situation?

Saint Jerome, Saint Catherine's Cathedral, Bethlehem, West Bank

35

A HEART TO KNOW GOD

"I WILL GIVE THEM A HEART TO KNOW ME, THAT I AM THE LORD. THEY WILL BE MY PEOPLE, AND I WILL BE THEIR GOD, FOR THEY WILL RETURN TO ME WITH ALL THEIR HEART." JEREMIAH 24:7

JESUS ANSWERED HER, "IF YOU KNEW THE GIFT OF GOD AND WHO IT IS THAT ASKS YOU FOR A DRINK, YOU WOULD HAVE ASKED HIM AND HE WOULD HAVE GIVEN YOU LIVING WATER." JOHN 4:10

Western Wall of Second Jewish Temple, Jerusalem, Israel

God provides an amazing promise through Jeremiah. I long to have a heart that knows God. At times I feel as if I am growing in the right direction, but at other times I sense distance between God and myself – I feel spiritually disconnected. I know God is present, but in those times I am not and I have an unfulfilled longing in my soul. Have you experienced this? Is your soul thirsty? Do you long for fulfillment?

One day Jesus relaxed on sand near some water. He sat near a well in Samaria waiting on a woman to arrive. She arrived at noon. She did not know Him, but He knew her. He knew her history and her spiritual needs. He knew her soul was thirsty. Jesus asked her for a drink and He mentioned this amazing stuff that He called living water – spiritual sustenance leading to life eternal, life abundant. He told her it would remove her soul's thirst. At a later time in Jerusalem, Jesus described living water to crowds of people and John provided an editorial comment explaining that by "living water," Jesus meant the Holy Spirit.[3]

We know the Holy Spirit is a gift from God who is with us and in us.[4] We know the Holy Spirit is the Advisor, Counselor and Advocate who comes upon all who accept Jesus as Lord.[5] Jesus said the Holy Spirit will teach us all things and will guide us to truth.[6] God's holy word tells us that the Holy Spirit transforms our minds[7], conveys God's wisdom to us[8], and makes Christ's mind available to us[9]. One of Jesus' purposes is to provide abundant life for us,[10] which is delivered through the Holy Spirit.

---

[3] John 7:38-39
[4] Luke 11:13, John 14:15-17, Acts 1:4-5
[5] John 14:16, John 7:37-39, Galatians 3:1-5
[6] John 14:26, John 16:13
[7] Romans 8:1-17
[8] 1 Corinthians 2:6-16
[9] Id
[10] John 10:10

The Holy Spirit begins working on people before they believe and He never stops urging us closer to Christ. But other forces distract us like our busy lives, our continuous access to and constant need for entertainment and social media, and others. If we are constantly exclusively plugged into the world our connection with God will be diminished. God urges us, well He commands us, to respect the Sabbath, which means to rest, to spend time communing with God, and to spend time with others in the community of faith. We need rest, God and each other.

During the Last Supper Jesus says His farewell to the disciples.[11] He explains that He is about to leave them to go to the Father. After once again conveying this potentially disturbing news, He urges them not to be troubled because Jesus is preparing a place for them in the Father's house, and He will send His Holy Spirit to dwell with them and within them. Jesus explains that the Father dwells within Jesus and Jesus dwells within the Father and Jesus does the Father's works and speaks the Father's words and through the indwelling Holy Spirit believers will enjoy the same connection with Jesus as He enjoys with the Father. Jesus dwells within us through His Holy Spirit.

Through Jeremiah, God promises, "I will give them a heart to know me, that I am the Lord. They will be my people, and I will be their God, for they will return to me with all their heart." Through the unity of the Holy Trinity – Father, Son and Holy Spirit being one God – and His dwelling within us, He transforms our hearts to truly know Him.

Is your soul thirsty? Daily consumption of living water is the cure. I pray that we each reconnect or stay connected with the Holy Spirit through prayer, through God's holy word and through friends in faith. God promises to give you a heart to know Him. May you receive His holy gift.

---

[11] See John 13-16, with particular attention to John 14

THOUGHTS TO CONSIDER

1. Read Ezekiel 14. Through the prophet Ezekiel, God say,

> "Son of man, these men have set up idols in their hearts and put wicked stumbling blocks before their faces.... When any of the Israelites or any alien living in Israel separates himself from me and sets up idols in their hearts and puts a wicked stumbling block before his face and then goes to a prophet to inquire of me, I the Lord will answer him myself. I will set my face against that man and make him an example and a byword." Ezekiel 14:3 & 7-8

God says that the people "set up idols in their hearts" and separate themselves from God. The people make choices that create separation. What choices are you making that possibly create separation between you and God? Would you characterize any of the choices as "idols" or "stumbling blocks"? Why or why not?

2. Read Matthew 12:33-37. Jesus says, "Make a tree good and its fruit will be good ... For out of the overflow of the heart the mouth speaks" (Matthew 12:33-34). Our words reflect the condition of our hearts. Consider the words you speak. What do they reveal about the condition of your heart?

3. Read John 14. In this portion of His Farewell Discourse, what does He say about the connection between God the Father, Jesus, the Holy Spirit and

us? What do His promises mean to you? How do they influence your view of yourself?

4.   Read 1 Corinthians 2. God's holy word says,

> The Spirit searches all things, even the deep things of God. For who among men knows the thoughts of a man except the man's spirit within him? In the same way no one knows the thoughts of God except the Spirit of God.... But we have the mind of Christ. 1 Corinthians 2:10-11 & 16

When do you feel closest to God? What are you doing when you experience Him? What do you do each day to strengthen your connection with Him?

Qumran, West Bank

36

PEACE BE WITH YOU

"ALL THIS I HAVE SPOKEN WHILE STILL WITH YOU. BUT THE COUNSELOR, THE HOLY SPIRIT, WHOM THE FATHER WILL SEND IN MY NAME, WILL TEACH YOU ALL THINGS AND WILL REMIND YOU OF EVERYTHING I HAVE SAID TO YOU. PEACE I LEAVE WITH YOU; MY PEACE I GIVE YOU. I DO NOT GIVE TO YOU AS THE WORLD GIVES. DO NOT LET YOUR HEARTS BE TROUBLED AND DO NOT BE AFRAID." JOHN 14:25-27

"YOU BELIEVE AT LAST!" JESUS ANSWERED. "BUT A TIME IS COMING, AND HAS COME, WHEN YOU WILL BE SCATTERED, EACH TO HIS OWN HOME. YOU WILL LEAVE ME ALL ALONE. YET I AM NOT ALONE, FOR MY FATHER IS WITH ME. I HAVE TOLD YOU THESE THINGS, SO THAT IN ME YOU MAY HAVE PEACE. IN THIS WORLD YOU WILL HAVE TROUBLE. BUT TAKE HEART! I HAVE OVERCOME THE WORLD." JOHN 16:31-33

AGAIN JESUS SAID, "PEACE BE WITH YOU! AS THE FATHER HAS SENT ME, I AM SENDING YOU." AND WITH THAT HE BREATHED ON THEM AND SAID, "RECEIVE THE HOLY SPIRIT." JOHN 20:21-22

During the Last Supper, Jesus teaches about the Holy Spirit and foretells many of the events that would soon occur. He wants the disciples to understand that the events, as horrific as they would be, were all part of God's greater plan, so that they will have peace through that knowledge and in Jesus Christ. Jesus promises the Holy Spirit and says, "Peace I leave with you; my peace I give you" and urges his listeners to put away their fears.

Nonetheless, the disciples are troubled, they grieve and they are afraid. They are unable to appreciate the events swirling around them. Not long after the first Easter, as the disciples meet behind locked doors because they fear religious leaders, suddenly, Jesus appears in all His post-resurrection glory. Displaying wounds as evidence of His identity He says, "Peace be with you! ... Receive the Holy Spirit."

In three short sentences He issues two commands. He appears in love. He reveals His wounds to prove His identity and His love, and He instructs the disciples to accept His peace and to receive the Holy Spirit. Peace and the Holy Spirit flow together.

On an earlier occasion, Jesus said, "Come to me, all you who are weary and burdened, and I will give you rest" (Matthew 11:28). While He continues to offer peace, rest and the elimination of weariness and burdens as a gift, we must go to Him, we must seek Him, and we must accept His gift of holy grace. And we often miss out.

I recently read an article posing a theory about people in the United States today. The author says that we see abundance of money as a status symbol and abundance of time as shameful. The theory suggests that our culture demands that we continuously appear to be busy and it possibly explains why we tend to fill our discretionary time with activities. It also initiates a conversation regarding why we are willing to take on unnecessary debt to acquire unnecessary objects, acquiring the appearance of status and continuing our cycle of activity.

Are we culturally programmed to look busy? If so, this possibly explains our desire to participate in Bible studies, our desire to participate in mission work (which are both excellent things to desire by the way) and our aversion to prayer meetings. While prayer warriors know they are doing their mightiest work while praying, outsiders may see them praying and conclude they are merely sitting there with shamefully too much time on their hands. Does our culturally programmed need to be busy impact our faith lives?

Jesus calls us to receive His rest, to receive His peace, to receive the Holy Spirit. Certainly He calls us to serve, to know His holy word, to pray, to love one another, and to do many other activities, but our lives must be lived in balance with His rest and peace. He does not call us to busyness for the sake of appearance, rather He calls us to love one another, accept His peace and receive the Holy Spirit.

He is breathing on you. Inhale His peace. Inhale the Holy Spirit. As you breathe in, receive Him in a new and refreshed way.

Thoughts to Consider

1.   Read Matthew 11:28-30. Jesus promises rest to all weary and burdened people who "come to" Him. He continues saying, "Take my yoke upon you and learn from me, for I am gentle and humble in heart, and you will find rest for your souls" (Matthew 11:29). In verse 28 Jesus promises rest to those who "come to me" and in verse 29 He promises rest to those who take his yoke and learn from Him. How does taking His yoke and learning from Him relate to "coming to" Jesus? They both lead to gaining His rest, but are they equivalent?   Many religious leaders approached Jesus and engaged in conversation with Him, yet they did not "come to" Jesus in the sense that led to

experiencing His rest. So, the notion of "coming to" Jesus means more than merely approaching Him. If we are to receive His rest, we must surrender to Him, allow His holy transformation of our spirits and souls, and receive His spiritual sustenance that is His rest.

2. Read John 6:22-40. In this passage Jesus uses the same terminology, namely "He who comes to me ..." Jesus says, "I am the bread of life. He who comes to me will never go hungry, and he who believes in me will never be thirsty. But as I told you, you have seen me and still you do not believe" (John 6:35-36). Again, many people approached Jesus and listened to Him and engaged in conversation with Him, but left hungry and thirsty. Satisfaction requires spiritual transformation. He is the bread of life, consume Him daily, receive His holy transformation of your spirit and soul, accept His gift of satisfaction, wholeness and abundance.

3. Read Psalm 39. What is the source of David's emptiness? What is the source of his peace? What parallels do you see in your experience?

4. What is one thing you might do each day this week to discover Jesus Christ's peace in a new and refreshed way? What must you change in your life to allow that to happen?

37

Touching the Fringe

As he went, the crowds pressed in on him. Now there was a woman who had been suffering from hemorrhages for twelve years; and though she had spent all she had on physicians, no one could cure her. She came up behind him and touched the fringe of his clothes, and immediately her hemorrhage stopped. Then Jesus asked, "Who touched me?" When all denied it, Peter said, "Master, the crowds surround you and press in on you." But Jesus said, "Someone touched me; for I noticed that power had gone out from me." When the woman saw that she could not remain hidden, she came trembling; and falling down before him, she declared in the presence of all the people why she had touched him, and how she had been immediately healed. He said to her, "Daughter, your faith has made you well; go in peace." Luke 8:42-48 (NRSV)

For years the woman had suffered with a physical ailment physicians could not cure. She knew in her heart that Jesus could heal her and, if she only touched His cloak, Jesus would heal her. She saw Him and, seizing her opportunity, she touched His clothing and she was immediately healed. Do you believe events like that continue to happen today? Do you believe that Jesus Christ continues to offer physical healing to people today?

Duc in Altum, Magdala, Israel

If you believe that Jesus had the authority and power to perform the acts described in Scripture, if you believe that Jesus died and rose again, if you believe that Jesus ascended to heaven, if you believe it is the same Jesus who walked the earth that sits in heaven, if you believe that Jesus has all authority in heaven and on earth, if you believe that Jesus loves us and loves you, if you believe all that, do you believe that He continues to reach into our world and influence events today? Do you believe that God reveals His glory through miracles today?

We do not need to look very far to see people who have been touched by His holy healing hand, who Jesus has healed physically, spiritually, emotionally, psychologically. We just need to look around at people around us. He regularly reaches into our world and reveals His glory, but we need eyes to see.

On one particular Sunday I was not scheduled to teach Sunday school, so I took extra time after the early worship service talking with friends in the Sanctuary and hallways before slowly making my way to the Sunday school classrooms on the third floor. It was about 10:15 when I reached the top of the stairs.

Just as I did, the doors to the elevator opened revealing Pat Johnson. She asked if I had time to talk with her. I explained that, as strange as it was on a Sunday morning, I had time. Her left pupil was completely dilated making her left eyeball black. She explained that the night before she completely lost sight in the eye. That morning she saw a doctor who diagnosed her condition as central retinal vein occlusion – her main retinal vein was blocked. The doctor said no treatment is available to unblock the vein, she would not regain sight in the eye and she should receive monthly injections in the eye to prevent other problems from developing.

Pat asked if I would accompany her into the Genesis Sunday school class, interrupt the class, and ask everyone to pray for God to heal her eye. She asked specifically for me to pray for total and complete physical and spiritual healing for her, and for the Holy Spirit to transform our church and each individual in it.

A dozen or so of us prayed. We gathered around Pat, placed hands on her, anointed her with oil and prayed. Later that day she was able to see with the eye, but her vision was cloudy. I saw her the following Wednesday evening at our prayer meeting and her vision was almost back to normal. The following week she returned to her doctor. He said the injections that he previously recommended were no longer necessary. Her eye was back to normal.

God healed her eye in response to prayer. It was a rare occurrence for me to be free on a Sunday morning. It was a rare occurrence for me to be at that place at that time. But I just happened to arrive at the top of the stairs exactly when the elevator door opened. We had a divine appointment and God revealed His glory.

Do you believe that God reveals His glory through miracles today? We merely need to look around us to see evidence of His holy healing touch.

Thoughts to Consider

1. What is your honest, immediate response to the story about Pat? We are forced to stay continuously on guard as we live our lives in and seek to understand this world. At times trusted news outlets publish accounts inconsistent with one another and others flood the Internet with inaccurate information regarding the same events, causing us to question what really happened or worse, to give up the effort altogether. If we click on the wrong email thieves gain control of our computer. If we give the wrong bit of information over the phone thieves steal our identity. Through technology, thieves have gained access to our inner sanctums, forcing us to stay on guard as never before. We are forced to be skeptical about every bit of information we encounter. So I understand that you may be skeptical about the story above, but do you believe that God continues to reach into our world and act in response to our prayers? Why or why not?

2. Do you believe that God places people in our path to act as His servants as we travel through our days? I know that He does. I also know that from an early age we are taught to maintain our distance from strangers and to proceed with great caution encounter people we do not know. How should we maintain appropriate caution while opening

ourselves to God's plan to reveal His glory through people around us?

3. Read Mark 9. Jesus, Peter, James and John travel up Mount Hermon where they meet Elijah and Moses, God the Father speaks to them and Jesus is transfigured. After this amazing experience they descend the mountain. When they meet back with the other disciples they encounter a crowd surrounding a man and his demon-possessed son. The man asks Jesus to heal his son. During their conversation the man says, "I do believe; help me overcome my unbelief!" (Mark 9:24). How often do you pray a similar prayer?

4. Read Luke 10. Consider all the accounts in Scripture of Jesus and the apostles healing people. When Jesus sent out 72 missionaries, He instructed them saying, "When you enter a town and are welcomed, eat what is set before you. Heal the sick who are there and tell them, 'The kingdom of God is near you'" (Luke 10:8-9). We see many examples in Scripture of God working through His people in amazing ways, including physical healing. Do you see any place in Scripture where God says that sort of occurrence has stopped?

38

SEIZING THE POWER OF GOD

"FINALLY, BE STRONG IN THE LORD AND IN THE STRENGTH OF HIS POWER. PUT ON THE WHOLE ARMOR OF GOD, SO THAT YOU MAY BE ABLE TO STAND AGAINST THE WILES OF THE DEVIL. FOR OUR STRUGGLE IS NOT AGAINST ENEMIES OF BLOOD AND FLESH, BUT AGAINST THE RULERS, AGAINST THE AUTHORITIES, AGAINST THE COSMIC POWERS OF THIS PRESENT DARKNESS, AGAINST THE SPIRITUAL FORCES OF EVIL IN THE HEAVENLY PLACES" EPHESIANS 6:10-12 (NRSV).

Arch stone, Ephesus, Turkey

Using images typically reserved for warfare, God's holy word explains that evil spiritual forces attack us. Scripture also tells us what to do to protect ourselves – we must simply make use of the power and armor that God grants us to use.

With great eloquence, Paul describes our world as a dark place where we struggle against spiritual attack from evil forces, and he describes Godly defenses available to us. He presumes we will be attacked, but he does not presume that we know about God's defenses. In fact, it is with great urgency that Paul pleads with us to gain knowledge of the defenses available, to "be strong in the Lord and in the strength of his power," to "put on the whole armor of God," and to "stand against the wiles of the devil."

While God makes His strength, power and armor available, it is up to us to discover them, to deploy them and to stand. We must be strong, we must put on the armor, we must engage in resistance, we must struggle, we must act, we must seize the benefits of God's holy grace.

What does this mean? How are we to find strength in God's power?

Scripture describes Jesus frequently interacting with evil spirits. They engage in conversations, and the evil spirits know who Jesus is and submit to His authority. Jesus teaches that He gives believers authority over evil forces. In chapter 10 of his gospel, Luke describes a post-battle celebration. Jesus sent out seventy-two missionaries to preach the gospel. As they return they ware overjoyed to report that demons submitted to them in Jesus' name. Jesus explains, "See, I have given you authority to tread on snakes and scorpions, and over all the power of the enemy; and nothing will hurt you" (Luke 10:19). Jesus is not surprised by their encounters with demons, nor with the authority they possessed when dealing with demons. He merely explains the authority that He had granted them and then gently rebukes them for the seeds of pride sprouting, revealed through their joyful celebration. Jesus says, "I have given you authority … to overcome all the power of the enemy… However do not rejoice that the spirits submit to you, but rejoice that your names are written in heaven" (Luke 10:19-20).

As Jesus speaks to the seventy-two, He discusses authority over the enemy. Later He discusses power. Just before ascending to heaven, Jesus says, "But you will receive power when the Holy Spirit comes upon you…" (Acts 1:8).

We face a wily adversary with lots of experience – he was attacking, deceiving, manipulating and destroying people long before we were born. But we have authority granted by God connected to our relationship with Jesus Christ and the power of the Holy Spirit's indwelling. God grants power and authority, and Paul urges us to "be strong in the Lord and in the strength of His power." When you struggle with attack, please know you are not alone. Please know that God is with you and He provides for your defense, but we must each stand, put on the armor, be strong and seize God's power and authority.

Peter writes,

> Humble yourselves, therefore, under God's mighty hand, that he may lift you up in due time. Cast all your anxiety on him because he cares for you. Be self-controlled and alert. Your enemy the devil prowls around like a roaring lion looking for someone to devour. Resist him, standing firm in the faith, because you know that the family of believers throughout the world is undergoing the same kind of sufferings. 1 Peter 5:6-9

And James writes,

> Submit yourselves, then, to God. Resist the devil, and he will flee from you. Come near to God and he will come near to you. James 4:7-8

Peter and James each urge us to resist the devil. We surrender ourselves in humility to God and through faith, with the power and authority God gives us, we must stand firm resisting the devil. Satan will attack, but God is with us, giving us what we need when we need it, but it is up to each of us to stand and resist.

May you know in the depths of your soul that you truly possess His power and strength, may you stand firm in the confidence of your faith, may you trust in the victory of His truth.

Church of All Nations, Mount of Olives, Jerusalem, Israel

THOUGHTS TO CONSIDER

1.   When we think of evil in the world around us, we often think of distant events described in headlines involving people we do not know like suicide bombers, innocent people fleeing violence in lawless places, children huddling in war-torn villages without food or water, villages ravaged by a seemingly incurable virus, people losing every material possession from flood or fire or storm … the list could easily go on. When you think of evil in the world, what do you think of?

2.   When and how have you experienced "the wiles of the devil"? In those times, what did you do to repel the attacks?

3.   Describe times when you experienced God's power. What did it feel, smell and taste like?

4.   Read Ephesians 6:10-20. What specific steps will you take this week to receive more of God's holy power within you? As you establish your plan, please consider including lots of prayer and time delving into God's holy word. His word is the sword, which is useful both offensively and defensively.   Prayer is the umbrella under which everything is protected.

39

PROGRESSING TO CHILDLIKE

"PEOPLE WERE BRINGING LITTLE CHILDREN TO JESUS FOR HIM TO HAVE HIM TOUCH THEM, BUT THE DISCIPLES REBUKED THEM. WHEN JESUS SAW THIS, HE WAS INDIGNANT. HE SAID TO THEM, 'LET THE LITTLE CHILDREN COME TO ME, AND DO NOT HINDER THEM, FOR THE KINGDOM OF GOD BELONGS TO SUCH AS THESE. I TELL YOU THE TRUTH, ANYONE WHO WILL NOT RECEIVE THE KINGDOM OF GOD LIKE A LITTLE CHILD WILL NEVER ENTER IT.' AND HE TOOK THE CHILDREN IN HIS ARMS, PLACED HIS HANDS ON THEM AND BLESSED THEM." MARK 10:13-16

A friend recently described something I had written as "intellectual." I interpreted the words as positive, thinking that I must have sounded smarter than I am. Later that day another friend described her desire to allow her spirit to dominate her mind and body. She discussed her understanding that the Holy Spirit dwells within our spirit; our souls are gradually being transformed through contact with the Holy Spirit within us; but by focusing on our intellect and allowing our mind to control ourselves we hinder the Holy Spirit's transformative power.

As my friend spoke, I thought about the passage above and suddenly the label of "intellectual" felt far less positive. Is my need, my desire, my inclination to analyze hindering me from the fullness of life abundant available through the indwelling Holy Spirit?

When Jesus says, "I tell you the truth…" He is explaining that the words He is about to speak are extremely important. This is Jesus code for "If you have been daydreaming, its time to listen because what I am about to say is really important." With that introduction, Jesus says, "anyone who will not receive the kingdom of God like a little child will never enter it."

"Receive the kingdom of God like a little child." For me, in that moment, the words meant that I should simply receive the gift without over-analyzing it, and that I should drop the intellectual pretense and simply receive the gift thankfully. It meant that I need to progress from intellectual to childlike.

And while that may be true, intellect and childlike faith are not necessarily opposed to one another. We each possess a mind that is a gift from God. He created us in His holy image. He is all knowing. His ability to reason is perfect. He knows everything, so he never needs to extrapolate or project or otherwise fill in informational gaps. And He gives us our intellectual strength so that He might deploy each of us out in the world as His people accomplishing His unique plans.

Think about Paul. As Saul, he was raised in a well connected home in Tarsus. His father was Jewish but he gained favor with the Roman authorities gaining Roman citizenship for his family. So Paul likely interacted at the highest levels of Roman society in Tarsus, and then he went to Jerusalem to study under the leading Jewish scholar there. So he was well connected socially, intelligent, and driven to learn. He was also equipped to lead. He possessed the authority and privilege of Roman citizenship, he knew the Jewish law and customs, Roman law and customs, the languages and customs of the region, and God used all of this to employ Paul into His holy service. As Paul preached the Good News of Jesus Christ, he first artfully engaged his listeners to establish common ground. God did not call Paul to extinguish his intellectual capacity, He called Paul to use all of his experiences, all of his knowledge and the benefits of all his education combined with the other gifts God had bestowed upon him, all to reveal God's glory.

Boat Chapel, Magdala, Israel

And so it is with us. Intellectual strength is not necessarily opposed to childlike faith. God gives each of us certain gifts, talents and experiences so that He might reveal His glory through them. Each day, we are each being called into His glorious service in a unique way. In one of his letters to the church in Corinth, Paul writes,

> There are different kinds of gifts, but the same Spirit. There are different kinds of service, but the same Lord. There are different kinds of working, but the same God works all of them in all men.

> Now to each one the manifestation of the Spirit is given for the common good. To one there is given through the Spirit a message of wisdom, to another a message of knowledge by means of the same Spirit, to another faith by the same Spirit, to another gifts of healing by that one Spirit, to another miraculous powers, to another prophesy, to another distinguishing between spirits, to another speaking in different kinds of tongues, and still to another the interpretation of tongues. All these are the work of one and the same Spirit, and he gives them to each one, just as he determines. 1 Corinthians 12:4-11

Intellectual capacity is a gift from God that we should use for His glory. Wrestling with God's holy word is a wonderful thing to do. God presents His holy word as a means of connecting with us and we should strive to commune with Him as fully as possible through His word, employing all our intellectual capacity, as limited as it might be. However, if we are not careful, if we focus our intellect exclusively on matters from the world around us, it may hinder our lives of faith.

So how do we embrace and strengthen and employ intellectual power while moving towards childlike faith? In his letter to the church in Rome, Paul writes,

> Therefore, I urge you, brothers, in view of God's mercy, to offer your bodies as living sacrifices, holy and pleasing to God – this is your spiritual act of worship. Do not conform any longer to the pattern of this world, but be transformed by the renewing of your mind. Then you will be able to test and approve what God's will is – his good, pleasing and perfect will. Romans 12:1-2

Through childlike faith we accept holy mysteries that we will never fully comprehend. We accept that God's ways are not our ways and His mind is infinitely greater than our minds and His knowledge and capacity for thought are infinite and ours are certainly limited. Through faith we surrender ourselves completely to God, allowing His holy indwelling to consume us. Through faith we allow Him to transform our minds, but we do not lose our intellect in the process; rather, we gain His power to use our intellect and all the other gifts He bestows upon each of us to His glory. It is all for His glory.

May you continue to allow God's glory to be revealed through you.

THOUGHTS TO CONSIDER

1. Have you experience intellectual attacks on your faith? What was the setting? Who initiated the attack? What were the elements of the intellectual argument? How did you respond? How did it influence you?

2. Have you heard it said that faith is blind or that people of faith abandon rational thought? How do you respond to statements such as those?

3. What does childlike faith look like?

4. What will you do to seek the kingdom of God through childlike faith this week? How will your priorities change to accommodate this mission?

Cathedral of the Annunciation, Nazareth, Israel

40

LIVES OF OUR WORDS

"THEN I SAW THE LAMB, LOOKING AS IF IT HAD BEEN SLAIN, STANDING AT THE CENTER OF THE THRONE, ENCIRCLED BY THE FOUR LIVING CREATURES AND THE ELDERS. THE LAMB HAD SEVEN HORNS AND SEVEN EYES, WHICH ARE THE SEVEN SPIRITS OF GOD SENT OUT INTO ALL THE EARTH. HE CAME AND TOOK THE SCROLL FROM THE RIGHT HAND OF HIM WHO SAT ON THE THRONE. AND WHEN HE HAD TAKEN IT, THE FOUR LIVING CREATURES AND THE TWENTY-FOUR ELDERS FELL DOWN BEFORE THE LAMB. EACH ONE HAD A HARP AND THEY WERE HOLDING GOLDEN BOWLS FULL OF INCENSE, WHICH ARE THE PRAYERS OF THE SAINTS." REVELATION 5:6-8

Monastery of Zoodochos of Pigi, Patmos, Greece

Scripture tells us that our prayers live in heaven long after we pray. I love the image of heavenly beings carrying golden bowls filled with our prayers and treating them with sacred reverence. This suggests that when we speak, something is created – our prayers are sacred creations lingering like fragrant incense long after we speak.

What about other words we choose to speak? Do they continue to live after we speak them?

Scripture tells us that (i) God created all things by speaking, [12] indicating that His words have amazing creative power beyond our ability to imagine; (ii) people are created in God's image; [13] (iii) Jesus is God; [14] and (iv) Jesus grants us a portion of His authority and power [15]. If we possess a portion of God's image and some portion of His power and authority, do we speak things into existence? After we speak, do our words continue with lives of their own like ripples in a pond? If they do, what sort of creation are we leaving in our wake?

Words say something about the speaker and they influence each person who encounters them. When we read or hear words and allow the thoughts communicated through them to enter our consciousness, they alter us. Once information enters our mind we are forever changed. The change may be good or bad, or it may simply be the loss of a little of our storage capacity, but change is a certainty. Once a word is unleashed it cannot be taken back. Neither speaker nor listener can unring the bell.

In this sense, our words may not linger like prayers held in golden bowls, but they do live on in the lives of people who are changed by them. What sort of impact do you have on others? Is it holy, pure, peaceful? Does it build unity?

---

[12] See Genesis 1
[13] See Genesis 1:26-27
[14] John 1:1-5
[15] Luke 10:19

Entrance to Cave of the Apocalypse, Patmos, Greece

In his epistle, James spends a great deal of energy discussing our tongues and the mayhem they are capable of causing. He writes,

> If anyone considers himself religious and yet does not keep a tight rein on his tongue, he deceives himself and his religion is worthless.... With the tongue we praise our Lord and Father, and with it we curse men, who have been made in God's likeness. Out of the same mouth come praise and cursing. My brothers, this should not be. Can both fresh water and salt water flow from the same spring? James 1:26 & 3:9-11

And Jesus teaches that while we should be concerned with our words, we should be more concerned about the condition of our spirits and souls, because corrupted hearts produce ugly, dishonest and unkind words. Our words merely reveal who we really are and are often symptoms of deeper problems.

As Jesus spars with religious leaders about traditions regarding ceremonial cleansing, He quotes Isaiah 29:13 accusing them of honoring God with their lips while their hearts are distant from God. After leaving the religious leaders, Jesus shares the following conversation with the disciples. Jesus says,

> "Every plant that my heavenly Father has not planted will be pulled up by the roots. Leave them; they are blind guides. If the blind lead the blind, both will fall into a pit." Peter said, "Explain the parable to us."

> "Are you so dull?" Jesus asked them. "Don't you see that whatever enters the mouth goes into the stomach and then out of the body? But the things that come out of the mouth come from the heart, and these make a man 'unclean.' For out of the heart come evil thoughts – murder, adultery, sexual immorality, theft, false testimony, slander. These are what make a man 'unclean'; but eating with unwashed hands does not make him 'unclean.'" Matthew 15:13-20

As with much of His teaching, Jesus focuses on inner purity. He urges us to seek spiritual transformation available in Him through the indwelling Holy Spirit and continue progressing along the path towards holiness. He urges us to be His beacons of light, allowing His light to fill us and flow through us illuminating the dark world around us. He urges us to allow Him to reveal His glory to the world through us.

Imagine your words as seeds of transformation. Do your words reflect God's light, life and love? May God's glory be revealed through you and your words.

Thoughts to Consider

1.   Read Revelation 4 & 5. Imagine John kneeling in a cave on the island Patmos praying, when suddenly he was able to see heaven.   He was no longer looking at walls of a cave illuminated by candles. He peered into heaven and he saw amazing heavenly beings praising and worshiping God and doing remarkable things. As he tries to describe heavenly things our human minds and language are barriers to his efforts to communicate the wonders of the vision before him – I imagine it must have been difficult for him to communicate heavenly visions using earthly images.   How does John's account, including his description of heavenly beings holding golden bowls filled with incense that is the prayers of God's people, influence your view of your prayers?

2.   Read John 8:12-20. Jesus says, "I am the light of the world. Whoever follows me will never walk in darkness, but will have the light of life" (John 8:12). Jesus is light and His followers have the light of life. How have you experienced His light?

3.   Read Matthew 5:13-16. Jesus says that you are salt and light. Jesus is light. He abides in you. Does His light flow through you illuminating the darkness around you?   Consider specific ways His light has been revealed to others through your words.

4. Jesus urges us to focus on our spiritual transformation available through relationship with

Him suggesting that true righteousness will be revealed through pure words, actions and lives. What will you do this week to intentionally seek God?

View from Dominus Flevit Church, Mount of Olives, Jerusalem, Israel

41

ENEMY'S ATTACK

"BE SELF-CONTROLLED AND ALERT. YOUR ENEMY
THE DEVIL PROWLS AROUND LIKE A ROARING LION
LOOKING FOR SOMEONE TO DEVOUR." 1 PETER 5:8

Gabriele Amorth, chief exorcist at the Vatican, believes that the devil seeks to devour everyone. He is not picking and choosing whom to attack; rather, he is analyzing each person locating the best place to attack. Each person has a soft spot, a weakness, a gap where the devil will find little resistance inserting his influence into their life. With this in mind, Amorth suggests that we read the passage from Peter as follows: Your enemy the devil prowls around like a roaring lion seeking *the best place* to devour you.[16]

I imagine the devil probing me, looking for my weaknesses. I am not a carpenter and the carpentry projects I have attempted have been somewhat disastrous, but I recall projects requiring that I locate a stud behind drywall. Experts can tap a wall with their fingertips, feeling and hearing the difference between drywall fixed to a stud and drywall spanning the hollow space between studs. By gently tapping they locate studs. I imagine the devil doing the same thing to me: gently tapping, watching my actions, looking for my points of weakness and attacking me there.

---

[16] Amorth, Gabrielle, *An Exorcist Explains the Demonic: The Antics of Satan and His Army of Fallen Angels.* Sophia Press Institute (2016). ISBN 9781622823451.

Where will the devil find little resistance getting a foothold in your life, allowing him to continuously distract you from God and the truth? While the possibilities are endless, they often result from our choices. I urge you to take a personal inventory, assess your weak points, consider doors you may have opened in your life allowing the devil in, and when you see one, repent, pray for strength to turn away from it, and hate it enough to ban it from your life to shut the door.

As John the Baptist paved the way for the coming Messiah, he preached a message of repentance saying, "Repent, for the kingdom of heaven is near" (Matthew 3:2). To repent means to turn around. It means to pay attention to the direction of our lives, and if we are heading in the wrong direction, to recognize it, stop, turn to face the goal and proceed towards the goal. If we are facing the wrong direction and we continue racing forward, no matter how much time and energy we use, we will not make progress. If our goal is God and relationship with Him, then we should begin by facing Him and then move towards Him.

I recall one particular family vacation road trip as a boy. I do not recall how old I was, but I was old enough to read a map and still young enough for my father to question whether I could. He had driven the route many times, but before the trip, he gave me an atlas and asked me to help him navigate. We left early in the morning, really in the middle of the night, when my father could drive and the rest of us would sleep.

After driving for hours, he stopped at a café somewhere in Kansas and woke us up for breakfast. As we left, I pulled out the map to see where we were. I found the town we ate in and the route heading west to Colorado, and as we passed various markers I looked for them on the map but did not see them. I could not locate marker after marker. We crossed a river and I looked for the river on the map and saw that our route should not cross that river. Then I found roads crossing the river and looked for the markers seen earlier and sure enough, they were on the map, but not along the route we should have been traveling.

I told my father we were going the wrong direction. He ignored me. I explained that we should not have crossed the river we had just crossed, and he continued to ignore me. Finally, I asked him to tell me the highway number that we should be traveling. He told me and the next time we passed a sign identifying the road we were traveling, he realized that we were on the wrong road. So we stopped, turned around and went back to a place where we could get on the right path.

We usually think that to progress we must keep moving. But if we are moving in the wrong direction, stopping is the beginning of progress.

Satan is probing you; he is testing you, analyzing your responses, looking for your points of weakness. What tempts you? Jesus teaches us to pray "And lead us not into temptation, but deliver us from the evil one" (Matthew 6:13). If we were not tempted and if we never needed deliverance, Jesus would not teach us to pray that prayer. We are each tempted and we need deliverance and once we overcome one form of temptation a new one will arise. We must stay continuously vigilant because the enemy continues to prowl like a lion.

As we progress towards God, when our movement stalls we should pray for guidance, for wisdom, for God's discerning spirit, for eyes to see obstacles in our path, and for the strength and courage to remove obstacles once they are identified. And if we discover a facet of our lives leading away from God, we must stop, turn around, face God and move toward Him – we must repent.

Stand on the power and authority God gives you, trust in His strength, have faith that His promises are true, continue to study His holy word, and pray.

Saint Peter's Square, Vatican City

THOUGHTS TO CONSIDER

1.   Read 1 Peter 5. Peter reminds us that he was an eyewitness to the sufferings of Jesus Christ.   He traveled with Jesus, ate with Jesus, lived with Jesus, listened to His preaching and teaching, followed Jesus during His earthly ministry and witnessed the miraculous signs and wonders that God performed through Him. Peter then writes, "Humble yourselves, therefore, under God's mighty hand, that he may lift you up in due time. Cast all your anxiety on him, because he cares for you" (1 Peter 5:6-7).

Immediately after writing those words, Peter writes the sentence first set forth above, warning us about Satan prowling like a lion. He reminds us about his relationship with Christ Jesus, urges us to be humble, urges us to cast all our anxiety on Him, then warns about Satan's attacks. How do humility and surrender relate to being alert and sober and resisting the enemy's attacks?

2. Do you agree with Father Amorth's interpretation of 1 Peter 5:8? Why or why not?

3. What doors have you opened in your life allowing the enemy's attacks? What will you do to remove the enemy from your life and seal the door?

4. Think of Satan's efforts to tempt you. What did he do? How did you respond? What will you do in preparation for his next episode of tempting?

Walking path between Cana and Capernaum, Israel

42

"Do Whatever He Tells You"

ON THE THIRD DAY A WEDDING TOOK PLACE AT CANA IN GALILEE. JESUS' MOTHER WAS THERE, AND JESUS AND HIS DISCIPLES HAD ALSO BEEN INVITED TO THE WEDDING. WHEN THE WINE WAS GONE, JESUS' MOTHER SAID TO HIM, "THEY HAVE NO MORE WINE." "DEAR WOMAN, WHY DO YOU INVOLVE ME?" JESUS REPLIED. "MY TIME HAS NOT YET COME." HIS MOTHER SAID TO THE SERVANTS, "DO WHATEVER HE TELLS YOU." JOHN 2:1-5

We know the story well. Jesus instructs unnamed servants to fill six large stone vessels, each capable of holding twenty to thirty gallons, with water. After they do so, Jesus asks one of the servants to take a sample from one of the jars to the master of the ceremony who tastes it and proclaims it to be the best wine served during the celebration. This was "the first of his miraculous signs ... He thus revealed his glory and his disciples put their faith in him" (John 2:11).

By faith, Mary set the events in motion. She informed Jesus of the problem; she instructed servants standing nearby to follow Jesus' instructions; and she stood aside to allow the events to unfold. Had she seen Him do things like this in the past, her prodding would be easily understood, but Scripture says this was "the first of his miraculous signs," meaning she had not seen Jesus do anything like this before. She had faith in Jesus, in His calling, in His anointing, in who God made Him to be. And like a good mother bird, she shoved Him out of the nest forcing Him to spread His wings to fly.

The servants merely followed orders. They did as they were instructed and by doing so they participated in the miracle, but they did not act out of faith. While they participated out of a sense of duty, not faith, I imagine the miracle captured their attention and faith possibly followed.

What is Jesus calling you to do today? Like the unnamed servants who helped Jesus convert water into wine, perhaps we are somewhat lacking in our faith. The beauty is that we do not necessarily need faith to serve Him. We simply need to "do whatever he tells [us]." When we do and we see Jesus reveal His glory, our faith will grow.

May you hear His call, may you have the courage and strength to follow His instruction, and may God continue to reveal His glory through you.

THOUGHTS TO CONSIDER

1. Read Luke 1:26-56. Mary initiated the entire event. She prodded Jesus to act and she organized the servants to follow His orders. How did she know in her heart that Jesus could and should do this particular act? We know that the Holy Spirit had "come upon" her (see Luke 1:35) and performed the miraculous sign of Jesus' virgin birth through her, so Mary had been intertwined with the Holy Spirit for at least thirty years when she felt the call to prod Jesus into action. She undoubtedly was prompted by the Holy Spirit to act, but why did He involve her?

2.   Read John 14. The words Jesus speaks are His Father's words and the works He does are His Father's works. Jesus says,

> "Don't you know me, Philip, even after I have been among you such a long time? Anyone who has seen me has seen the Father. How can you say, 'Show us the Father'? Don't you believe that I am in the Father, and that the Father is in me? The words that I say to you are not just my own. Rather it is the Father, living in me, who is doing his work. Believe me when I say that I am in the Father and the Father is in me; or at least believe on the evidence of the miracles themselves." John 14:9-11

As you ponder Jesus' first miraculous sign and Mary's prodding and the servants' participation, consider the fact that Jesus' works are the Father's. It was God the Father working through Jesus who caused the miracle.   Does this change your perspective on the miracle itself or the roles of each participant? How so?

3.   Read John 21. Jesus turned water into wine as His first miraculous sign of God's glory flowing through Him.   He concluded His earthly ministry with a miraculous catch of fish and by calling Peter to dedicate the rest of his life serving Jesus. How are His call and miraculous signs and wonders connected in your experience with Him?

4.   During the course of His ministry Jesus performed countless more acts and miraculous signs and

wonders. John concludes his gospel writing, "Jesus did many other things as well. If every one of them were written down, I suppose that even the whole world would not have room for the books that would be written" (John 21:25).

The Synagogue Church, Nazareth, Israel

43

NEW LIFE IN CHRIST

SO THEN, PUTTING AWAY FALSEHOOD, LET ALL OF US SPEAK THE TRUTH TO OUR NEIGHBORS, FOR WE ARE MEMBERS OF ONE ANOTHER. BE ANGRY BUT DO NOT SIN; DO NOT LET THE SUN GO DOWN ON YOUR ANGER, AND DO NOT MAKE ROOM FOR THE DEVIL. THIEVES MUST GIVE UP STEALING; RATHER LET THEM LABOR AND WORK HONESTLY WITH THEIR OWN HANDS, SO AS TO HAVE SOMETHING TO SHARE WITH THE NEEDY. LET NO EVIL TALK COME OUT OF YOUR MOUTHS, BUT ONLY WHAT IS USEFUL FOR BUILDING UP, AS THERE IS NEED, SO YOU'RE YOUR WORDS MAY GIVE GRACE TO THOSE WHO HEAR. AND DO NOT GRIEVE THE HOLY SPIRIT OF GOD, WITH WHICH YOU WERE MARKED WITH A SEAL FOR THE DAY OF REDEMPTION. PUT AWAY FROM YOU ALL BITTERNESS AND WRATH AND ANGER AND WRANGLING AND SLANDER, TOGETHER WITH ALL MALICE, AND BE KIND TO ONE ANOTHER, TENDERHEARTED, FORGIVING ONE ANOTHER, AS GOD IN CHRIST HAS FORGIVEN YOU. THEREFORE, BE IMITATORS OF GOD, AS BELOVED CHILDREN, AND LIVE IN LOVE, AS CHRIST LOVED US AND GAVE HIMSELF UP FOR US, A FRAGRANT OFFERING AND SACRIFICE TO GOD. EPHESIANS 4:25-32 AND 5:1-2 (NRSV)

Jesus came to change the world and He urges us to be His holy agents of transformation. He wants to transform us so that we can help Him transform the world. He urges us to be in the world but not of the world. This suggests that (i) the world is in need of change, (ii) as Jesus' followers we have been changed, and (iii) He wants to act in the world through us.

Mosaic floor in Church of the Beatitudes by the Sea of Galilee, Israel

While Jesus says our transformation in Christ begins when we are "born of the Spirit" (John 3:8), Paul discusses it as new life in Christ. After urging his readers to embrace their unique skills, passions and gifts, and to work together as one body of Christ building unity and love, he contrasts new life in Christ with old life of the dark, selfish world (see Ephesians 4). He describes unbelievers as living "in the futility of their minds … darkened in their understanding; alienated from the life of God because of their ignorance and hardness of heart"

(Ephesians 4:17-18, NRSV). He urges his readers to leave their old way of life, to pursue righteousness and holiness in Jesus Christ, and to be "renewed in the spirit of your minds" (Ephesians 4:23, NRSV).

Anticipating questions, Paul provides specific examples to clarify what he means. He says to replace bitterness, wrath, anger, slander and malice with kindness, love, compassion and forgiveness. He says not to lie, tell the truth, and when we get angry, patch things up quickly – "Do not let the sun go down on your anger, and do not make room for the devil" (Ephesians 4:26-27, NRSV).

He urges us to speak only words of grace and to be imitators of God. As we strive to achieve these lofty goals we continue living our lives submerged in the world, and culture, society, people and the devil continue to influence us. Christ Jesus dwells within us and we are being transformed by His holy presence and while God calls us to transform the world, we are also being influenced by it. At what point do worldly influences taint our values, sway our character and distract us from being the people God calls us to be? If we change too much in response to wordly influence, will we revert back to the darkness of our old lives and no longer be salt and light? Paul provides a glimpse of what the old life looks like. It looks bitter, angry and tainted by evil.

Writing to Christians, Paul warns "and do not make room for the devil." The indwelling Holy Spirit characterizes new life in Christ, but the devil continues to attack, so we need to be on guard against unholy influences.

Jesus came to change the world (see Matthew 10:34-35, 1 John 3:8, Hebrews 2:14) and He calls us to be His agents of change, light in the darkness, and flavor in an otherwise bland world. As children of God, we need to be people through whom He transforms the world in which we live. As we are out in the world, we should allow His love, grace, mercy, light and life to flow through us, revealing His glory to everyone with eyes to see. May God's glory continue to shine through you.

View of Sea of Galilee from Church of the Beatitudes, Israel

THOUGHTS TO CONSIDER

1. Do you believe God created you for a purpose? Are you living a life consistent with that purpose?

2. Recognizing that God, through His holy word, calls you to be an imitator of Him, what needs to change in your daily pattern of living? What will you do this week to begin effectuating the changes necessary?

3. Recall the most recent time you were angry. How did you seek reconciliation? Did your anger "make room for the devil"? How will you handle similar situations differently in the future?

4. As you ponder the goals presented in the Scripture reading above, as lofty as they are, please know that Jesus Christ and the Holy Spirit dwells within you beginning the moment you accept Christ as your Savior. The power of the Holy Spirit fills you. His angels lift you up and protect you. Please know that you are not alone. Pray for His peace, His rest, His strength, His power, and His holy anointing on you and your life, and He will help you as you move forward along the path towards Him.

44

TRUST, FAITH & PEACE

"YOU WILL KEEP IN PERFECT PEACE HIM WHOSE MIND IS STEADFAST, BECAUSE HE TRUSTS IN YOU. TRUST IN THE LORD FOREVER, FOR THE LORD, THE LORD, IS THE ROCK ETERNAL." ISAIAH 26:3-4

Caves at Qumran, West Bank

Isaiah records a song of praise as chapter 26. The quote above includes two lines of the song connecting trust and peace. When we trust in God, He keeps us in His perfect peace.

A frequently used illustration of trust involves a tightrope walker. In 1859, a French acrobat named Jean Francois Gravelet, also known as Charles Blondin, and the Great Blondin, advertised that he would string a rope across Niagara gorge, just below Niagara Falls, and walk the 1,300-foot stretch.[17] On June 30, 1859, he was delighted that crowds gathered to watch the event and his delight grew as people placed bets with one another regarding whether he would successfully cross the span or plunge to his death. He carried a 26-foot ash pole as he stepped off land in the United States and continued walking until he once again reached land, this time in Canada. After making the journey across, he returned carrying a large box camera on his back, stopping to photograph the crowd. Two weeks later he repeated the walk to Canada across the rope. As he prepared to return to the United States walking the same rope, he picked up a wheelbarrow. Legend has it that he asked the crowd in Canada whether they believed he would successfully cross the span once again, they all cheered, "Yes!" Then he asked, "Does anyone want to ride in the wheelbarrow?" He had no takers.

They had seen evidence of his ability, they believed he would accomplish the feat once again, but no one trusted enough to place his or her life in his hands, or rather, his feet. At what point does belief turn into trust and faith?

Trust is the basis of faith. The Hebrew word translated as faith, aman, means "to be true" or "to be trustworthy." The root word means "solid" or "firm." Faith is certainty that the

---

[17] Abbott, Karen, "The Daredevil of Niagara Falls," Smithsonian (October 18, 2011)

one upon whom faith is placed is solid, firm and worthy of trust. Trust and faith are related, but while we place trust in many things as we chart our daily lives (for instance we trust that approaching cars will stay in their lane), the basis of our faith is God and God is the source of our faith. Paul writes in many different ways that our faith is a gift from God. He writes, "… in accordance with the measure of faith God has given you" (Romans 12:3). He describes faith and peace as characteristics of fruit of the Spirit saying, "But the fruit of the Spirit is love, joy, peace, patience, kindness, goodness, faithfulness, gentleness and self-control" (Galatians 5:22-23). He also explains that faith comes from hearing the message about Jesus Christ (see Romans 10:17).

Faith is a gift from God. Trust is a component of faith. Trust in God leads to peace.

What causes you to worry, makes you anxious, keeps you awake at night? Do you believe in your heart that God created all things by speaking? Do you believe that He created you and He breathes the breath of life into you? Do you believe that God has all authority in heaven and on earth, He is sovereign, and He knows everything, including everything that you need and desire? Do you believe that He is love, He loves you, and He desires relationship with you? If you believe all that, do you trust Him to act? Do you trust that He will act in such a way that His love, His glory, His holiness will be revealed. If you trust, if you have complete confidence and faith that His promises are true and that He is worthy of your trust, He promises to provide perfect peace.

I love the way that sounds. Perfect peace. With all that in mind, why do we worry?

Isn't worry an indication that we do not really trust? "But the fruit of the Spirit is … peace, … faithfulness, …." As we allow the Holy Spirit to roam around in our lives, our spirits and our souls, His fruit, His peace and His faith grow within us.

As Isaiah writes in his song of praise to God, "You will keep in perfect peace him whose mind is steadfast, because he trusts in you."

May you find God's perfect peace. May His glory shine upon you, may His Holy Spirit invade you, fill you and flow through you, and may you share His peace with the world.

Thoughts to Consider

1. Describe a time when God has asked you to get in His wheelbarrow. What gave you the confidence to trust Him?

2. In your experience, when have you known perfect peace? How is your experience with perfect peace connected with faith and trust?

3. Read Romans 10. Paul writes to the church in Rome agonizing about his fellow Jews who are zealous for God, who have heard the message about Jesus Christ, but do not believe in Jesus Christ. They lack faith. He concludes the chapter quoting the prophet Isaiah writing, "All day long I have held out my hands to a disobedient and obstinate people" (Romans 10:21). Do you see any parallel between your faith, revealed by your trust, and the folks that Paul describes in chapter 10?

4. Read Isaiah 25-26. Isaiah begins writing, "Oh Lord, you are my God; I will exalt you and praise your name, for in perfect faithfulness you have done marvelous things, things planned long ago" (Isaiah 25:1). Describe the wonderful things God has done

for you. How does your recollection of the evidence of God's faithfulness influence your faith and trust?

Dead Sea, West Bank

45

Sifted Like Wheat

"Simon, Simon, Satan has asked to sift you as wheat. But I have prayed for you, Simon, that your faith may not fail. And when you have turned back, strengthen your brothers."

But he replied, "Lord, I am ready to go with you to prison and to death."

Jesus answered, "I tell you, Peter, before the rooster crows today, you will deny three times that you know me."

Then Jesus asked them, "When I sent you without purse, bag or sandal, did you lack anything?"

"Nothing," they answered.

He said to them, "But now if you have a purse, take it, and also a bag; and if you don't have a sword, sell your cloak and buy one. It is written: 'And he was numbered with the transgressors;' and I tell you that this must be fulfilled in me. Yes, what is written about me is reaching its fulfillment."

The disciples said, "See, Lord, here are two swords."

"That is enough," he replied. Luke 22:31-38

Peter's Denial, Caiaphas' Palace, Jerusalem, Israel

What chaos is swirling around your life at the moment? What is ripping you apart on the inside, causing anxiety and sleepless nights? Jesus refers to this as being sifted like wheat, the process of ripping grain from stalk, separating the desired nugget from what will soon be discarded as waste.

During the Last Supper, Jesus warns that Satan is about to test Peter's faith. Satan asked for permission to do so. Jesus prays for Peter, He prays that Peter's faith will stay strong, but He does not seek to cancel Satan's authority to sift. Peter responds with confidence in his loyalty and dedication, but Jesus knows that the test heading Peter's way is an entirely new sort of test.

Jesus continues His tone of warning, telling the disciples to obtain swords because a time is coming when they would need them. Shortly after this conversation, the sifting begins. Guards arrive to arrest Jesus; disciples draw their swords and strike a guard removing his ear. Jesus heals the man and orders everyone to put away his sword (see Luke 22:47-54).

Peter witnesses Jesus as He is taken into custody and his worldview is suddenly thrown into chaos. He had been confident that Jesus was the Messiah, but he expects the Messiah to conquer, not submit, and his faith is tested. The events swirling around him do not conform with his expectations. As a result, he denies knowing Jesus, returns to Galilee and resumes his old job and old life.

But Jesus tracks Peter down, restores fellowship with him and calls him to lead His church. A few weeks later, the Holy Spirit fills Peter and, at tremendous personal risk, he stands in Jerusalem preaching the good news of Jesus Christ. 3,000 people come to know Jesus in response to Peter's first sermon. Jesus prayed that Peter's faith would not fail and that he would strengthen his brothers, and His prayer was answered.

Sifting separates the desired nugget from waste. If wheat had feelings, it would undoubtedly be a painful process, but the results are life giving. Peter's faith was tested and in response to being sifted he grew stronger than ever.

Is Satan sifting you like wheat? Like Peter, has your life been suddenly turned upside down? Is your faith being tested? Please know that Jesus is with you, He is praying for you and your faith, and He will position you so that the changes you are experiencing will reveal God's glory.

May your faith remain strong, may you know in your heart that God is with you, and may you grow stronger through the things you are experiencing.

Church of the Primacy of Saint Peter, Tabgha, Israel

ndy L. Allen

THOUGHTS TO CONSIDER

1.   Are events swirling around you that are shattering your expectations? Is it possible that God is granting Satan authority to sift you as wheat?

2.   How did Peter respond to his time of sifting? What do you think he did correctly? What might he have done differently?   How will you respond to your sifting?   How does Peter's example influence your plan moving forward?

3.   Do you believe that Jesus is praying for you? How does this influence your thinking on this matter?

4.   Read Matthew 5:1-12. Jesus promises His special blessing on people while they are experiencing times of difficulty.   How does this promise fit with the concept of Satan sifting?

4

46

GOD PROVIDES ABUNDANCE

"SHE WENT AWAY AND DID AS ELIJAH HAD TOLD HER.
SO THERE WAS FOOD EVERY DAY FOR ELIJAH AND FOR
THE WOMAN AND HER FAMILY. FOR THE JAR OF FLOUR
WAS NOT USED UP AND THE JUG OF OIL DID NOT RUN DRY,
IN KEEPING WITH THE WORD OF THE LORD SPOKEN BY
ELIJAH." 1 KINGS 17:15-16

What is testing your faith? Is a situation in your life causing you to surrender? Or possibly you see a need and you feel called to offer help out of the resources God has blessed you as steward over. Scripture reveals that our faith may be tested when we have too little to satisfy our needs, and also when we have enough.

When drought came, God sent Elijah north to Zarephath saying that a widow there would provide food for him. When Elijah arrived, he spoke with a woman who was gathering sticks. He asked her for food and water. She said she had only enough flour and oil for a small loaf. In fact, she was gathering sticks to make her last loaf, which she planned to eat with her son before dying. She had given up and was preparing to die. Elijah told her that God told him that if she made a loaf for Elijah, she would have enough for herself and her son also, and her provisions would not be used up. She trusted. She did as Elijah instructed and God continued providing flour and oil, the jars did not go empty (see 1 Kings 17). The woman acted in faith. In response, God accepted her offering and satisfied her needs.

Over 800 years later, a large crowd of people followed Jesus to the far side of the Sea of Galilee. A boy gave his dinner to Jesus, who prayed over it, divided it into baskets and distributed it to the crowd. Thousands of people ate until they were satisfied and leftovers filled twelve baskets (see John 6:1-15). The boy acted in faith. In response, God accepted his offering and provided abundance.

Church of the Multiplication, Tabgha, Israel

As we read stories like these in Scripture, we sometimes forget that they describe real people. The woman in Zarephath was a living person who had surrendered her life believing she would soon starve to death. Through her surrender she trusted Elijah and God, and acted in faith.

The boy was in the opposite situation. He had what he needed. He was fully prepared, yet surrounded by people in need. Rather than minding his own business and enjoying his meal, he acted with compassion through faith.

What is testing your faith today? After the boy and the woman acted through faith, God provided abundance. The act of faith came first. If we trust God and act in faith with what we have, He is able to make it more than it could ever be on its own. God provides abundance.

May you have new eyes to see, may you experience Him deeply within your soul, may your heart be fertile soil for His seeds to grow, may you step out in faith and receive His abundant grace showering over you.

Synagogue, Capernaum, Israel

Thoughts to Consider

1.   Read 1 Kings 17. He was God's holy spokesperson on earth. He said what God instructed him to say. When his life was threatened because of what he said, God did not repel the attack, rather, he told Elijah to run. How was Elijah's faith tested in the events described in chapter 17?

2. If God is truly all-powerful with all authority in heaven and on earth, why did He not simply remove the threat to Elijah's life?

3.   How was the woman's faith tested? How did she demonstrate faith? What parallels exist in your life?

4. Read John 6:1-15.   How was the boy's faith tested? What parallels exist in your life?

47

TRUSTING FUTURE PROVISION

NOW FAITH IS BEING SURE OF WHAT WE HOPE FOR AND CERTAIN OF WHAT WE DO NOT SEE. THIS IS WHAT THE ANCIENTS WERE COMMENDED FOR. BY FAITH WE UNDERSTAND THAT THE UNIVERSE WAS FORMED AT GOD'S COMMAND, SO THAT WHAT IS SEEN WAS NOT MADE OUT OF WHAT WAS VISIBLE. BY FAITH ABEL OFFERED GOD A BETTER SACRIFICE THAN CAIN DID. BY FAITH HE WAS COMMENDED AS A RIGHTEOUS MAN, WHEN GOD SPOKE WELL OF HIS OFFERINGS. AND BY FAITH HE STILL SPEAKS, EVEN THOUGH HE IS DEAD....

BY FAITH NOAH, WHEN WARNED ABOUT THINGS NOT YET SEEN, IN HOLY FEAR BUILT AN ARK TO SAVE HIS FAMILY. BY HIS FAITH HE CONDEMNED THE WORLD AND BECAME HEIR OF THE RIGHTEOUSNESS THAT COMES BY FAITH.

BY FAITH ABRAHAM, WHEN CALLED TO GO TO A PLACE HE WOULD LATER RECEIVE AS HIS INHERITANCE, OBEYED AND WENT, EVEN THOUGH HE DID NOT KNOW WHERE HE WAS GOING. BY FAITH HE MADE HIS HOME IN THE PROMISED LAND LIKE A STRANGER IN A FOREIGN COUNTRY; HE LIVED IN TENTS, AS DID ISAAC AND JACOB, WHO WERE HEIRS WITH HIM OF THE SAME PROMISE. FOR HE WAS LOOKING FORWARD TO THE CITY WITH FOUNDATIONS, WHOSE ARCHITECT AND BUILDER IS GOD. BY FAITH ABRAHAM, EVEN THOUGH HE WAS PAST AGE — AND SARAH HERSELF WAS BARREN — WAS ENABLED TO BECOME A FATHER BECAUSE HE

CONSIDERED HIM FAITHFUL WHO HAD MADE THE
PROMISE. AND SO FROM THIS ONE MAN, AND HE AS
GOOD AS DEAD, CAME DESCENDANTS AS NUMEROUS
AS THE STARS IN THE SKY AND AS COUNTLESS AS THE SAND
ON THE SEASHORE. HEBREWS 11:1-4 AND 7-12

Sphere Within a Sphere, Vatican Museums, Vatican City

Faith involves confidence, hope and assurance. We often use the word "hope" in reference to a desire, no matter how unlikely it might be. Students who fail to study for an exam may hope the questions only cover things they know. A person buying a lottery ticket hopes he or she will win. But that is not how the word "hope" is used in the passage above. In the passage, hope is expectation that the future event will occur, like expecting the sun will rise tomorrow.

Faith is confidence, absolute trust that God will satisfy our expectations based on His promises. Faith is knowing in my heart with certainty that God is really real, that He really acts in my life, that He really loves me, and that He provides for me. As I look back over my life, I can connect certain dots as evidence of His hand at work. Looking backward, faith is relatively easy, but faith is really about maintaining confidence looking forward. Faith is trusting that He will continue to provide in the future, and showing our trust through action.

God recently blessed me with an unexpected opportunity to earn extra income. It was an opportunity that I never would have imagined, completely out of the blue, and it came at a time of need. It was definitely a gift from God. As I starting working, I knew exactly how I would thank God for His holy gift of grace. After I was paid for the work and the money sat in our account, I felt suddenly hesitant to follow through with my plans. I saw other needs on the horizon, and the thought entered my mind that I should keep God's portion in preparation for future needs. Even in response to tangible evidence of God's holy grace pouring over my life, my faith is pitifully weak.

If we fail to see God's glory shining around us and His holy grace showering over us, we miss faith affirming and faith strengthening opportunities. And even when we see Him acting in the past or present, we often fail to trust that He will continue to act in the future. Over and over in the Old Testament we see

God urging His people to put away their idols and trust Him. I doubt any of us worship statues as gods, but how often do we review our bank account and place our trust in the numbers we see? And when we see the numbers, do we see evidence of God's abundant provision or do we see evidence of our individual hard work and something that is all mine? Has the account become something that we place our trust in and possibly worship?

Acting today in a manner revealing our trust, hope and confidence that God will continue to provide in the future is the essence of faith. The writer of Hebrews discusses the faith of some people described in the Old Testament including Abel, Enoch, Noah, Abraham, Sarah and others. They believed God, they trusted God, the placed their confidence even when their circumstances were difficult. Noah continued building the ark while everyone around him mocked and ridiculed him. God promised to make Abraham into a great nation, even though he and his wife were past childbearing age, but they trusted God rather than the human view of their situation. Abraham packed up and left his home, following God, and for the remainder of his life lived in a tent "like a stranger in a foreign country" but the continued trusting God. And God delivered on His promise.

"Now faith is being sure of what we hope for and certain of what we do not see. This is what the ancients were commended for" (Hebrews 11:1-2). Faith is knowing in the depths of our souls and spirits that God is really with us and that His promises are true, even when our circumstances appear bleak through our human view of the situation.

May you have new eyes to see, may you experience Him deeply within your soul, may your heart be fertile soil for His seeds to grow, may you step out in faith, confidence and trust knowing that He will continue to provide.

THOUGHTS TO CONSIDER

1. Read Psalm 71. Psalm 71 says, "For you have been my hope, O Sovereign Lord, my confidence since my youth" (v.5) and "But as for me, I will always have hope; I will praise you more and more" (v.14). The psalmist describes God as his refuge, rescuer, deliverer, rock, fortress and hope. He describes God's faithfulness to him. How has God been faithful to you? What words would you use to describe His faithfulness to you?

2. Read 1 Thessalonians 1. Paul writes, "We continually remember before our God and Father your work produced by faith, your labor prompted by love, and your endurance inspired by hope in our Lord Jesus Christ" (1 Thessalonians 1:3). Consider how Paul weaves the concepts of faith, love and hope. As you read 1 Thessalonians, what concepts are being communicated by the words?

3. Read 1 Corinthians 13. Describe the ways Paul weaves the concepts of faith, hope and love in this passage. As you read the passage, what jumps out at you? Does anything surprise you?

4. Read Genesis 12-25. God calls Abram to leave his country and promises to make him into a great nation and bless him (see Genesis 12:1-2). Abram was 75 years old with no children. He packed up and left and followed God and endured many hardships along the way. When he was 99 years old, he was still childless (see 17:1). God promised that Sarah would have a son the following year (see 18:10), and

she did (see 21:1-7). Think about the time and hardship Abram/Abraham endured between the time of God's promise and Isaac's birth. How does this influence your view of God's faithfulness and our expectations?

Fields near Bethlehem, West Bank

48

SAYING THANK YOU

ONE OF THEM, WHEN HE SAW HE WAS HEALED,
CAME BACK, PRAISING GOD IN A LOUD VOICE. HE
THREW HIMSELF AT JESUS' FEET AND THANKED HIM – AND
HE WAS A SAMARITAN. LUKE 17:15-16

Sometimes I get busy with life and I fail to appreciate how awesome God is. I fail to consider His awesome power, authority, mercy, grace and love, and as a result, I fail to praise and thank Him.

The passage is part of a story describing Jesus healing ten people suffering with leprosy. As Jesus enters a village in the vicinity of Samaria and Galilee, a group of ten people, respecting the custom relating to their condition, maintain distance from Jesus while shouting, "Jesus, Master, have pity on us!" (Luke 17:13). Jesus sees them and simply instructs them to go to their priest to be pronounced clean. In response, they do as they are told – they start walking towards the synagogue. As they walk they are healed. One of them, as soon as he realizes his physical condition has changed, runs back to Jesus, throws himself at Jesus' feet, praises God and thanks Jesus.

Jesus says, "Were not all ten cleansed? Where are the other nine? Was no one found to return and give praise to God except this foreigner?" Then he said to him, "Rise and go; your faith has made you well" (Luke 17:17-19).

Randy L. Allen

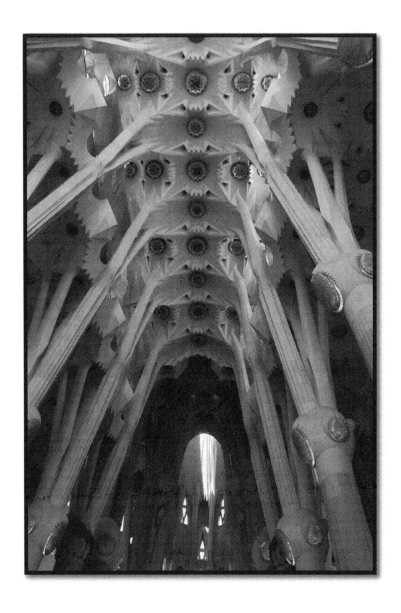

Basílica de la Sagrada Familia, Barcelona, Catalonia, Spain

Jesus connects faith and healing. They were all healed, they all possessed the faith necessary to receive God's blessing, yet only one returned to praise God and say, "thanks." Did the other nine, while basking in personal pleasure of their blessed state, suddenly forget the source of their blessing? Did they begin imagining a myriad of other rational explanations for their healing? Did they simply move past it and blindly continue along the path of their new life, or did they decide not to return to Jesus, choosing to follow His instructions instead (Jesus said, "Go, show yourselves to your priests" (v.14))? We can only imagine why, but 90% failed to thank Jesus for His compassion, mercy, grace and love, and failed to bow before Him acknowledging His power and authority.

As we see in most passages, the story has a number of interesting twists. In first century Holy Lands lepers were outcasts and untouchable. Many thought that God had cursed people with leprosy, and Jews saw Samaritans as outcasts, so a Samaritan leper was on the far fringe of society. Jesus' blessing is available to everyone, even people on the extreme fringe of society like a Samaritan leper. No matter who we are, no matter the condition of our life, no matter what we have done, no matter how society may see us, we are each eligible for God's blessing. God loves you. His holy grace is showering over you. Through faith we receive and open His gift of grace.

Jesus said to the one who returned to Him, "Your faith has made you well." Faith allows us to see God's hand at work, to realize what we have is the result of His blessing, to receive His healing, and to open His gift of grace. Faith heals.

How is He blessing you today? Do you see His holy hand at work in your life? Do you see evidence of his power, authority, mercy, grace and love surrounding you? If you do, praise His holy name and thank Him. If you do not, pray for God to enlighten the eyes of your spirit that you might see.

May you have new eyes to see, may you experience Him deeply within your soul, may your heart be fertile soil for His seeds to grow, may you step out in faith and receive His abundant grace showering over you.

THOUGHTS TO CONSIDER

1. Read Psalm 138. The psalm, attributed to King David, expresses praise and thanksgiving to God for His love, faithfulness, name, word and because He answers prayers. What specific blessings in your life do you thank God for? How do you express your praise and thanksgiving to God?

2. What is worship? Did the Samaritan leper worship Jesus? Did he worship God? Why or why not?

3. Jesus says, "Rise and go; your faith has made you well" (Luke 17:19). How did the man with leprosy demonstrate his faith? How do people around you see your faith in action?

4. As you think back over your life of faith, have you been more frequently like the nine or the one? How so? If you feel the need to change anything in your life in response to the passage above, what will you change?

49

DO NOT WORRY

"DO NOT WORRY ABOUT ANYTHING, BUT IN EVERYTHING BY PRAYER AND SUPPLICATION WITH THANKSGIVING LET YOUR REQUESTS BE MADE KNOWN TO GOD. AND THE PEACE OF GOD, WHICH SURPASSES ALL UNDERSTANDING, WILL GUARD YOUR HEARTS AND YOUR MINDS IN CHRIST JESUS." PHILIPPIANS 4:6-7 (NRSV)

A friend recently asked whether worry is a sin. Scripture repeatedly tells us not to worry. Jesus commands us not to worry (Matthew 6:25-34) and promises to take away our burdens and give us rest (Matthew 11:28-30). In the passage above Paul urges us not to worry. Peter also instructs us to give our worries to Jesus (1 Peter 5:7). While rest and loss of burdens sound tremendously better than worry, is worry a sin?

The question forces us to consider sin. God is the standard by which sin is determined. We often say that God can do anything and everything, but God cannot sin. It is impossible for God to sin because He is the standard. Sin is separation from God.

The realm in which we live is a place of great contrast. It is the place where evil roams and reveals itself; it is also the place where God showers His holy grace and reveals His glory. While living on earth, we are each separated from God. Even the holiest people you know are, to some extent, separated from God. Through His death and resurrection, Jesus provides a bridge connecting us with God. Each choice we make moves us either towards God or away from God. Choices enhancing our separation from Him are sinful.

So is worry a sin? Worry is a symptom of our separation from God. Worry reveals our lack of faith, our lack of trust, our lack of confidence that God is really with us, is really true to His word, and will really provide for us in the future. After commanding us not to worry, Jesus explains that God the Father knows our needs and Jesus completes the thought by saying, "But strive first for the kingdom of God and his righteousness, and all these things will be given you as well" (Matthew 6:33, NRSV). As we seek God and move closer to Him along the path towards sanctification, faith grows and worry diminishes.

Trust, confidence and hope grow out of faith, and faith reveals itself through our actions. God's holy words says,

> Therefore, brothers, since we have confidence to enter the Most Holy Place by the blood of Jesus, by a new and living way opened for us through the curtain, that is, his body, and since we have a great priest over the house of God, let us draw near to God with a sincere heart in full assurance of faith, having our hearts sprinkled to cleanse us from a guilty conscience and having our bodies washed with pure water. Let us hold unswervingly to the hope we profess, for he who promised is faithful. And let us consider how we may spur one another on toward love and good deeds. Let us not giving up meeting together, as some are in the habit of doing, but let us encourage one another – and all the more as you see the Day approaching. Hebrews 10:19-25

We have confidence in Christ Jesus, we trust that He is who He claims to be, and we believe His promises are true. With that in mind, "Let us hold unswervingly to the hope we profess, for he who promised is faithful." We trust, we hope, we have confidence, we sincerely believe and have faith, but at times, when faced with the onslaught of chaos, turbulence and risk the world delivers, our faith falters.

Worry reveals our lack of faith. May your confidence, trust and faith in Jesus Christ and the truth of His promises continuously grow. May God bless you with His comfort, His peace and His rest.

Bush that is, according to monastic tradition, *the* Burning Bush
Saint Catherine's Monastery, Mount Sinai, Egypt

Thoughts to Consider

1. Read 1 Peter 5. Peter instructs his readers to "humble yourselves, therefore, under God's mighty hand, that he may lift you up in due time" (1 Peter 5:6). He then says to "cast all your anxiety on [God] because he cares for you" (1 Peter 5:7). Immediately after saying that, Peter writes,

> Be self-controlled and alert. Your enemy the devil prowls around like a roaring lion looking for someone to devour. Resist him, standing firm in the faith, because you know that your brothers throughout the world are undergoing the same kind of sufferings. 1 Peter 5:8

In three consecutive sentences, Peter connects the thoughts of humility, trusting God and Satan's attack. In your experience, how are the three concepts connected?

2. Read Matthew 6. In chapters 5-7, Matthew records Jesus giving the Sermon on the Mount, so chapter 6 presents the middle of the sermon. Jesus discusses giving to people in need, He teaches about prayer, He discusses fasting and treasure in heaven, and then He says,

> "Therefore I tell you, do not worry about your life, what you will eat or drink; or about your body, what you will wear. Is not life more important than food, and the body more important than clothes? ... But seek first his kingdom and his righteousness, and all these

things will be given to you as well. Therefore do not worry about tomorrow, for tomorrow will worry about itself. Each day has enough trouble of its own." Matthew 6:25 & 33-34

How does this teaching relate to trust, confidence, hope and faith? Based on your experience, how does the level of worry in your life correspond to the amount of time you spend seeking God's kingdom and His righteousness? Should you change anything in your life?

3. Read Matthew 11. John the Baptist was related to Jesus and they knew each other. John the Baptist baptized Jesus and He heard God proclaim Jesus to be His Son. John the Baptist told his followers to follow Jesus because Jesus as the Messiah. So he believed in Jesus, but then he was imprisoned. He never saw Jesus preach or perform miracles or engage in His ministry, so as John the Baptist sat in prison he began to wonder whether Jesus is really the One. He sends friends to Jesus asking Him whether He is the One. Jesus responds, denounces towns that saw His miracles yet refused to repent, and then He prays an amazing prayer and teaches about His relationship and connection with God the Father, and then He says,

"Come to me, all you who are weary and burdened, and I will give you rest. Take my yoke upon you and learn from me, for I am gentle and humble in heart, and you will find rest for your souls. For my yoke is easy and my burden is light." Matthew 11:28-30

How does Jesus' response to John the Baptist relate to trust, confidence, hope and faith? Contrast His response to John the Baptist to his statements about Chorazin, Bethsaida and Capernaum. What did people in the towns do or fail to do that was so bad? Are we guilty of similar things?

What must we do to receive His rest?

4. Read Philippians 4. Paul begins chapter 4 by pleading with Euodia and Syntyche to discover unity and he asks his friends to help them do so. Immediately after this he commands us to rejoice, and to let our "gentleness be evident to all" (Philippians 4:5). He then writes the passage first set forth above commanding us not to worry. He connects removal of worry and anxiety to prayer and God's peace.

How does Paul's teaching compare with the teaching of Peter and Jesus mentioned above? What is similar? What is different? Based on the collection of teaching, do you see anything in your life that you need to change?

Wall of the Second Jewish Temple, Jerusalem, Israel

50

PRAYER INHIBITS TEMPTATION

"WATCH AND PRAY SO THAT YOU WILL NOT FALL INTO TEMPTATION. THE SPIRIT IS WILLING, BUT THE BODY IS WEAK." MATTHEW 26:41

We all struggle with temptation. When you feel yourself engaged in the struggle, pray because prayer inhibits temptation.

After the Last Supper as Jesus and the disciples entered the garden, Jesus asked His friends to pray with a specific purpose in mind – He suggested that they pray to prevent falling into temptation. To some extent, we are bifurcated beings. We are spirit, soul and body, and while the Holy Spirit dwells within our spirit the moment we first believe, it takes a little longer for His holiness to permeate the rest of our being. So long as we continue to live in this world, even though the Holy Spirit dwells within us, the world continues to attack.

Jesus mentioned flesh and spirit while suggesting that His friends pray. Our spirit represents the part of us in which God lives. Flesh represents the part of us not yet transformed by God's indwelling. Prayer is a state of being. It is opening our spirit to commune more fully with God. Viewed differently, it is one of the avenues through which we experience God, His presence, His holy grace. At first they seem like two views, but they quickly merge.

As I ponder the many aspects of prayer, I notice the light bulb lighting the room. I imagine the light bulb as spirit, electricity as the Holy Spirit, and the wire connecting the bulb to the energy source as prayer. Like the bulb, our spirit shines light when connected to the source of power. This is a poor analogy, as physical images depicting spiritual matters usually are, because the Holy Spirit enters our spirit upon belief. I mention it anyway because prayer strengthens the connection, brightens the glow, allows Him in more fully and enhances our transformation.

While in a prayerful state of being, we are insulated from spiritual attack and temptation diminishes. Prayer is an avenue through which the Holy Spirit enlightens the eyes of our spirit, helping us, with gradually increasing ability, to be sensitive to the world around us.

Jesus said, "Watch and pray so that you will not fall into temptation." Pray that you will not fall. Pray to inhibit temptation. May you be convicted, empowered and filled with the need and desire to follow His command.

Thoughts to Consider

1. Read Luke 4:1-13. Just after He was baptized in the Jordan River, Jesus was full of the Holy Spirit and the Holy Spirit led Him to the wilderness where Satan tempted Him. Satan tempted Jesus by pointing out His relationship with God the Father and suggesting that Jesus would use His power and authority to satisfy personal needs. Jesus chose to trust God the Father to provide for His needs. Next, Satan tempted Jesus by offering Him worldly glory in exchange for His relationship with God, but Jesus knew that God the Father is sovereign. Finally, Satan quotes Scripture and tempts Jesus to test God the Father by throwing Himself off a high place to see whether God the Father would really command His angels to save

Jesus. Satan accurately quoted the words of Scripture, but Jesus knew that Satan's use of Scripture was inconsistent with God's will. Jesus was "full of the Holy Spirit" (Luke 4:1) when He went to the wilderness and was tempted. How significant do you think that fact was? Based on your experience, how does the Holy Spirit help you when you are tempted?

2. Read James 1. James begins his epistle by discussing trials and temptation. As you read the chapter, what passage speaks most clearly to you? Why?

3. James explains, "the testing of your faith produces endurance; and let endurance have its full effect, so that you may be mature and complete, lacking in nothing" (James 1:2-4, NRSV). In your experience, how has testing of your faith produced endurance, maturity and complete faith?

4. Read Matthew 6:5-15. Jesus teaches us to pray, "And lead us not into temptation, but deliver us from the evil one" (Matthew 6:13). How does this prayer influence your understanding of temptation and the role of prayer regarding temptation?

Basilica de la Sagrada Familia, Barcelona, Catalonia, Spain

Randy L. Allen

51

PRUNING BRANCHES

"I AM THE TRUE VINE, AND MY FATHER IS THE VINEGROWER. HE REMOVES EVERY BRANCH IN ME THAT BEARS NO FRUIT. EVERY BRANCH THAT BEARS FRUIT HE PRUNES TO MAKE IT BEAR MORE FRUIT. YOU HAVE ALREADY BEEN CLEANSED BY THE WORD THAT I HAVE SPOKEN TO YOU. ABIDE IN ME AS I ABIDE IN YOU. JUST AS A BRANCH CANNOT BEAR FRUIT BY ITSELF UNLESS IT ABIDES IN THE VINE, NEITHER CAN YOU UNLESS YOU ABIDE IN ME." JOHN 15:1-4 (NRSV)

Caesarea Philippi, Israel

260

Some branches are connected to Jesus Christ yet bear no fruit. God the Father removes them. Other branches bear fruit and God the Father prunes them to make them more fruitful. Every branch endures the pain of being cut; the difference involves location and purpose.

Vines produce fruit for a season, and then are dormant in an annual cycle. Mature grapevines are pruned each winter. After branches shed their leaves, wood associated with the previous year's growth is removed. If branches are not pruned, they get too big and use up nutrients that would otherwise go to fruit. Overgrown, long branches are the ones that, while still connected to the vine, fail to produce good fruit. By pruning, branches are kept lean and strong, enabled them to produce a larger and better tasting crop because nutrients go into grapes.

The passage forces me to evaluate my life. What fruit is Jesus Christ producing through me? If I fail to see evidence of fruit, is this merely a dormant season or is it evidence of a larger problem? Have my needs become too large? Is my life consuming nutrients and resources designed to produce fruit? The next time the vinegrower passes by with His shears, will I be pruned or removed?

How is God pruning you? How is He preparing you to produce a better crop? Please know that the pruning you experience is for God's glorious purpose. May you continue to abide in Christ and He in you. May He continue to produce good fruit through you.

THOUGHTS TO CONSIDER

1.   Read John 15:1-17. The passage is taken from the incredible evening of teaching Jesus delivered during the Last Supper, which fills John 13-16. Jesus washes the disciples' feet teaching about loving service. He foretells His betrayal. He gives the new commandment saying, "Love one another. As I have loved you, so you must love one another" (John 13:34). He predicts Peter's denial, teaches that He is "the way, the truth and the life" (John 14:6), and promises the Holy Spirit. And then He describes Himself as "the true vine" (John 15:1). Given the full context of Jesus' teaching that evening, how do you see His directive for us to abide or remain in Him?

2.   God the Father is presented as the gardener who prunes and removes branches depending on the fruit produced through each branch. How does this image shape your understanding of God the Father? What surprises you about it?

3.   Jesus Christ is presented as the vine with His disciples presented as branches growing out of Him, abiding In Him. How does this image influence your view of Jesus Christ, of your relationship with Him, of the fruit produced through you?

4.   Given the teaching about pruning and removal, is there anything you feel the need to change in your life? What steps will you begin this week to begin your path of change?

52

PEACE IN CHRIST

"I HAVE TOLD YOU THESE THINGS, SO THAT IN ME YOU MAY HAVE PEACE. IN THIS WORLD YOU WILL HAVE TROUBLE. BUT TAKE HEART! I HAVE OVERCOME THE WORLD." JOHN 16:33

On the evening of the Last Supper Jesus taught lesson after lesson in rapid succession. He concludes by saying three striking things. First, He explains the goal of His teaching is to deliver the peace that is available in Him. Second, so long as we live in this world we will experience trouble. Third, Jesus has "overcome the world."

Jesus promises we will face trials, tribulation, hardships and persecution, but He also reminds us that He is in control, promises that in Him we may have peace, and urges us to move forward with confidence. I recently heard a woman give her testimony to a large audience. To explain that she had not been living a holy life, she mentioned a number of activities she formerly pursued. She then described the moment she realized her soul felt empty. In that instant a few lines of Scripture she had learned years earlier suddenly entered her mind, and the words spoke to her in an unexpected way. She suddenly knew in her heart that Jesus had died for her, and that He was the answer for her longing. Her encounter with Jesus was unexpectedly personal. For as long as she could remember, she had not felt peace, but suddenly, in the instant she saw Jesus with newly opened eyes, she felt whole and satisfied. She felt peace in Christ.

Jordan River

We know that Jesus possesses all authority in heaven and on earth (Matthew 28:18). We know that Jesus is God (John 1). We know through the creation story that God transforms chaos into order by the power of His spoken word (Genesis 1), and we know that Jesus calms storms (Matthew 8:23, Mark 4:35, Luke 8:22) and satisfies physical and spiritual needs of people He encounters. So we know He is capable of doing amazing things, at least in some impersonal abstract way, but do you believe in your heart that He will do things like that for you? He promises that He has overcome the world. Do you believe that He wants to use His power and authority to help you as you encounter the world? Do you believe it in a personal way?

Jesus urges each of us to move forward with confidence in His power. He promises "my peace I give *you* … in me *you* may have peace … *take heart!* I have overcome the world." His message is spoken to you. His power leads to your peace. While the world encourages and creates chaos, while the world causes pain and suffering, Jesus has overcome the world and He promises peace in Him. Allow Him to calm the storms of your life. Allow Him to create order from the chaos swirling around you. Receive His gift of peace.

May the eyes of your spirit be enlightened, may you encounter Jesus in a new personal way, may you receive His gift of peace.

Beit Shean, Israel

THOUGHTS TO CONSIDER

1. Read John 16. The chapter begins with Jesus saying, "All this I have told you so that you do not go astray" (John 16:1). It concludes with the passage first written above. Between the two statements of assurance, Jesus promises trouble, pain and persecution. He promises the Holy Spirit who will convict the world of its sin and guide us to truth and speak the words Jesus asks Him to speak saying, "I will send him to you" (John 16:7). Jesus also promises that God the Father "will give you whatever you ask in my name" (John 16:23).

I am confident you have experienced pain, hardship, suffering and trouble because the world we live in exposes each of us to them. In light of that certainty, Jesus promises the Holy Spirit and God the Father's attentiveness to our prayers. Think about your encounters with Jesus Christ. Describe how you have felt His peace.

2. Read Deuteronomy 8. Deuteronomy presents Moses' farewell address. As the Israelites camp on the Jordan River and prepare to cross into the Promised Land, Moses knows that he will not go with them. He is reminding them of everything to help them prepare for what is to come. In the middle of this long presentation Moses says,

"Remember the long way that the Lord your God has led you these forty years in the wilderness, in order to humble you, testing you to know what was in your heart, whether or not you would keep his commandments. He humbled you by letting you hunger, then by feeding you manna ... in order to make you understand that one does not live by bread alone, but by every word that comes from the mouth of the Lord." Deuteronomy 8:2-3 (NRSV)

Have your experiences of trouble, hardship and pain driven you closer to God, or away from Him? Describe your experience and your reaction to it. How does the passage from Deuteronomy influence your response to your pain, suffering and hardship?

3. Read John 14. With this reading we return to Jesus teaching during the Last Supper, a little earlier than the Scripture reading above. Jesus says,

"All this I have spoken while still with you. But the Counselor, the Holy Spirit, whom the Father will send in my name, will teach you all things and will remind you of everything I have said to you. Peace I leave with you; my peace I give you. I do not give to you as the world gives. Do not let your hearts be troubled and do not be afraid." John 14:25-27

Jesus promises His peace and urges us not to let our hearts experience trouble. As the world attacks, please know that His peace is with us. He is with you. His peace is personal to you.

4. Read Psalm 4. The psalmist concludes writing, "I will lie down and sleep in peace, for you alone, O Lord, make me dwell in safety" (Psalm 4:8). As you face the chaos of the world around you, how do you maintain your focus on God's assurances of protection and peace? What might you do today to keep your focus on God rather than the chaos?

Mineral Beach, Dead Sea, West Bank

Lori & Randy, Masada, Israel

ABOUT THE AUTHOR

Randy is husband to Lori, father to Elizabeth and Henry, fatherly to Meagan, and grandfather to Carson. He serves as associate pastor at First United Methodist Church in Tuscaloosa, Alabama and as managing partner of Druid Capital Partners in Northport, Alabama. His experience includes practicing law in Denver, Colorado, serving as general counsel to a privately owned company, launching and managing three private equity investment funds, serving on the board or in a board-like role to a dozen or so companies, serving as expert witness in court, testifying before legislative bodies, working as a ski lift operator at Beaver Creek, sweeping floors in a flour mill, working as a roustabout, and serving in all sorts of other interesting ways.

He enjoys quiet time with family, strolling on a Yolo board on Lake Tuscaloosa, participating in CrossFit over lunch, praying in the Sanctuary with close friends and strangers, praying alone in the backyard, and studying, talking about and writing about God's holy word.

In addition to completing courses to maintain his pastor's license, Randy holds a law degree from University of Colorado School of Law and an engineering degree from Colorado School of Mines.

Lori & Randy, Jerusalem, Israel

NOTES

If you would like to receive future devotionals please sign up for emails at

www.RandyLAllen.com

---

[i] Anderson, B.W., Bishop, S. and Newman, J.H., *Understanding the Old Testament*, 5th ed. Pearson Education, Inc. (2007, 1998).

[ii] See Exodus 22:21-22 and 23:6,9,11; Leviticus 25:6; and Deuteronomy 10:19 & 15:10-11.

[iii] This is a photo of a replica housed in an annex to St. Peter's Basilica. Dense crowds surrounded the original that day.

[iv] Leviticus 19:18

[v] Matthew 22:36-40, Mark 12:30-31

[vi] Ephesians 6:12

[vii] Colossians 1:13

[viii] 1 Peter 5:8

[ix] Luke 10:18

[x] Job 1:7 and 2:2

[xi] Matthew 5:13

[xii] Matthew 5:14-16

[xiii] "The United Methodist Hymnal: Book of United Methodist Worship." The United Methodist Publishing House, Nashville, Tennessee. P.10. (1989, 35th printing 2013).

[xiv] Id

[xv] Id

[xvi] See John 16:23-24, John 14:13-14 and Luke 10:19

[xvii] "Obama's Age of Discord," The Wall Street Journal, July 25, 2016, https://www.wsj.com/articles/obamas-age-of-discord-1469486668

Made in United States
Orlando, FL
02 March 2022

15278406R00154